Reay Country

REAY COUNTRY

The Story of a Sutherland Farming Family

Reay D. G. Clarke

ORIGIN

First published in 2014 by the Islands Book Trust
This second edition first published in 2018 by
Birlinn Origin, an imprint of
Birlinn Ltd
West Newington House
10 Newington Road
Edinburgh
EH9 1QS
www.birlinn.co.uk

ISBN: 978 1 91247 627 5

British Library Cataloguing in Publication Data
A catalogue record for this book is available from the British
Library

Printed and bound by Clays Ltd, Elcograf S.p.A.

Contents

Illustrations and Maps

Reay D. G. Clarke.

Reay D. G. Clarke: A Life Lived in, and for, the Highlands

James Hunter

Take the main road to Sutherland and Caithness from Inverness and, in under an hour, you cross the Beauly Firth, the Cromarty Firth and the Dornoch Firth. This is made possible by three imposing bridges. Completed between 1982 and 1991, those bridges, which have together transformed road travel in the Scottish north, are used daily by many thousands of people. While all sorts of individuals and institutions had a hand in their design, financing and construction, their existence is owed ultimately to one man. That man was this book's author, Reay Clarke. His insistence on the feasibility of what he called 'the crossing of the three firths' – in the face, to begin with, of scepticism and hostility from government and its agencies – originated in Reay's conviction that good planning starts with a commitment to good land use. That same conviction is apparent in this book. So too is Reay's belief that, in the Highlands, good land use has not been much in evidence for 200 or more years.

Reay Clarke died in Edderton Farm House on 17 May 2017. This was the Easter Ross home where he'd been born in 1923 and where, apart from time spent at boarding school and on military service, he'd always lived. My get-togethers with Reay, though they sometimes included trips across or around the Dornoch Firth and into Sutherland, always began with coffee and talk at a big and well-worn table in the farmhouse kitchen. It was at this same table, I discovered when researching these pages, that the case for spanning the Beauly, Cromarty and Dornoch Firths was first given shape.

The story begins with a 1968 letter preserved among a mass of correspondence, newspaper cuttings, research papers and other material filed away in the Edderton Farm office. This letter was sent to Reay by Inverness Royal Academy's then rector or head-teacher. Would Mr Clarke, the letter enquired, be good enough to speak on 'Land Usage' at a 'day conference' whose theme would be 'The Way Ahead for the Highlands'? Conference attendees, it was explained, would be senior students from secondary schools in Inverness and its surrounding area – from Kingussie at one end of this area to Tain at the other. Speakers, it was further ex-plained, would mostly be senior representatives of locally based public bodies. The principal such speaker would be Professor Robert Grieve, chairman of the Highlands and Islands Develop-ment Board (HIDB), an organisation then Scottish Secretary Willie Ross had set up three years earlier with a view to restoring prosperity to what had become one of the most run-down parts of Britain. Was the Royal Academy rector's approach to Reay in any way motivated by a hope that he might enliven the planned gathering by taking up positions at odds with those of the HIDB? Perhaps. Between Reay's take on Highland development and that of the HIDB's Robert Grieve there was certainly little in the way of overlap – something that become clear to Reay, he told me years afterwards, when he learned at first hand how Grieve felt about a proposal that his board back the restoration of farming families to one of the localities denuded of people in the course of the Highland Clearances.

That proposal originated in the work of the Highland Panel. This was a consultative grouping whose task, until the panel was disbanded on its role being taken over by the HIDB, was to advise government ministers on how best to deal with the north and its problems. The Highland Panel had been established in 1946. Although he would later become one of its members, its forma-tion is unlikely to have impinged greatly on the then 23-year-old Reay Clarke. His priorities in 1946 were wholly bound up with Edderton Farm to which he had just returned after five years in the wartime Royal Navy.

Active service for Reay began in September 1942 with his time on HMS Farndale, a destroyer he joined just prior to her leaving her south of England base for Loch Ewe on the Highland west coast – mustering point for British convoys bound for the Russian Arctic ports of Murmansk and Arkhangelsk. Long afterwards, in material he supplied to the Arctic Convoys Museum in Aultbea on the shores of Loch Ewe, Reay recalled his initial impressions of the convoy, codenamed PQ18, his ship was to join: 'It was a magnificent spectacle. The loch was crowded with merchant ships, the green fields of the crofts rose up from the shore and, on the eastern horizon, the Wester Ross mountains were outlined in red by the sunset.' What followed was less magnificent. During the three weeks it took to reach Arkhangelsk, more than a quarter of the 40-plus merchant ships making up PQ18 were sunk by enemy submarines and aircraft. Lives were lost. So was cargo after cargo of tanks, guns and other munitions intended for the Soviet Union's beleaguered Red Army – then engaged, like Britain's own forces, in a life-or-death struggle with Nazi Germany's Wehrmacht and Luftwaffe.

Not long out from Loch Ewe, PQ18 ran into an Atlantic storm which had the effect of dispersing its merchant vessels. 'We'd been despatched to gather some of the scattered ships,' Reay remembered, 'when a German submarine suddenly surfaced just astern of us. We attacked with gunfire, the submarine crash-dived and we followed up with depth charges. The submarine sustained some damage but was able to continue with her patrol, attacking the convoy again some days later.'

PQ18's course took the convoy into the Greenland Strait (its roundabout route into the Arctic Ocean being intended to keep its ships and their crews out of enemy bomber range for as long as possible) and then north around Iceland and on into the icy seas surrounding Bear Island. There Farndale was detached to escort a damaged merchant vessel back to the UK – in the teeth of a further storm so severe that the destroyer's starboard guard rails were stripped away by waves crashing over her decks.

Months earlier, when completing his initial training, Reay Clarke had applied to take an engineering course. On Farndale's return to Britain, he learned, by way of a telegraphed transfer order, that his application had been successful. Able Seaman Clarke, still only 19, was transformed, as a result, into Leading Mechanic Clarke prior to being sent to join a Bombay-based Motor Torpedo Boat Flotilla – the rest of Reay's time with the navy being spent, not in the Atlantic or Arctic Oceans, but in Indian and Burmese waters where Britain was at war with Imperial Japan.

The farm to which Reay Clarke came home from India in June 1946 was, at that stage, a not very extensive mix of arable and outrun located at the point where the flat fields bordering the Dornoch Firth's Ross-shire shore meet hill ground rising steeply to the south. This farm had first been been rented from Balnagown Estate in 1914 by Reay's father. He too was Reay – a name owed to that other farm, at Eriboll in north-west Sutherland's Reay Country, where Reay senior, like several of the other Clarkes whose stories are told in this book had been both born and raised.

Because the older Reay had died when his son was only eight, the younger Reay, this naval mechanic now turned young farmer, was confronted in the period immediately following the war with a place in urgent need of much care and attention. This Edderton Farm duly got. More land was acquired and improved; a 100-strong dairy herd was developed; milk bottled at Edderton was delivered daily to the nearby town of Tain; and, in the upland part of his now enlarged farm in what's known as Edderton Burn Glen, Reay set about the creation of the 400-acre woodland that was to be one of his most enduring passions. 'I have been a farmer all my life,' he wrote in 2005, 'but for just over 50 years now I have also been planting and tending my trees . . . There has been great satisfaction in the task.'

In 1950, Reay married Lydia Middleton. Soon there were four children at large in Edderton Farm House – Donald, Janey, Hugh and James. A young family, a dairy herd, a milk business and a steadily expanding forest might have served to keep most folk fully occupied. But not Reay. Increasingly, as the 1950s turned into the 1960s, he was drawn into active involvement in a wide range of organisations – the National Farmers Union of Scotland (NFUS), the North of Scotland Milk Marketing Board, a Forestry Commission advisory body, the Royal Scottish Forestry Society and, eventually, the Highland Panel. There Reay joined a number of key figures from across the Highlands and Islands – prominent among them Jo Grimond, Liberal MP for Orkney and Shetland, and Naomi Mitchison, Kintyre-based novelist, feminist, socialist and rural development activist. From people like these, Reay said, he received 'a valuable education in the politics, as opposed to the practicalities, of land use'.

Not long after the war, Reay had met and got to know the pioneer ecologist Frank Fraser Darling, then living in the North Argyll community of Strontian and working on the mammoth research project whose results inform Fraser Darling's 1955 publication, *West Highland Survey*. A comprehensive and path-breaking analysis of Highlands and Islands agricultural practice, demographics and much else, *West Highland Survey* was a book Reay valued greatly. His well-perused copy in one of Edderton Farm House's several laden bookcases still carries tags Reay used to mark favourite passages, not least sentences he reproduced in part in this book. From the concluding paragraph of Fraser Darling's introduction to the published version of his research findings, those sentences read: 'The foundations on which this Survey has been built are the soil, the sea and the natural resources on which the human population is dependent . . . And finally the bald, unpalatable fact is emphasised that the Highlands and Islands are largely a devastated terrain, and that any policy which ignores this fact cannot hope to achieve rehabilitation.'

It was thinking of this sort – thinking which coincided with his own – that Reay Clarke brought to the Highland Panel and, in particular, to the panel's concluding report. Entitled *Land Use in the Highlands and Islands*, this report was submitted at the end of October 1964 to Willie Ross who, days before, had been made Secretary of State for Scotland in Harold Wilson's newly-elected Labour government. 'We have the absolute obligation,' the Highland Panel insisted in a passage which bears Reay's imprint and which he underlined and annotated in his own copy of the panel's 1964 report, 'to see that the fertility of the soil . . . is steadily improved.' In much of the Highlands and Islands, as Fraser Darling had already stressed and as Reay was to emphasise over and over again, the opposite had for ages been happening over huge expanses that, in the post-clearance era, had first been given over to large-scale sheep farming and then, increasingly, to deer forest. It was with a view to reversing the ensuing loss of productivity and to 'arrest[ing] depopulation', that the Secretary of State should be prepared, the Highland Panel recommended, to use 'powers of compulsory acquisition' in order 'to bring into productive use underused land'. Among the localities where this might be done, or so it began to be suggested in late 1964 and early 1965, was the Strath of Kildonan, one of the several Sutherland valleys where community after community had been swept away in the course of the most notorious of all the Highland Clearances.

To start with, prospects for radical action of this kind looked good. In March 1965, in an impassioned House of Commons speech outlining the reasoning behind his planned Highlands and Islands Development Board, Willie Ross appeared to embrace the need for initiatives of exactly the sort advocated by the Highland Panel. 'Land is the basic resource of the Highlands and Islands,' the Scottish Secretary told MPs, 'and any plan for economic and social development would be meaningless if proper use of the land were not a part of it.' Although the Highland Panel's land use report, Reay said, had had to be 'watered down', as he put it, to make it acceptable to Scottish Office civil servants, he and others expected – in light of Willie Ross's Commons statements – the newly constituted HIDB, to whom Ross referred the panel's recommendations, to have land use high on its agenda. Nor was this expectation in any way undermined by the HIDB's own public stance on the Strath of Kildonan. Because of its close association with the 'history of the clearances', coupled with the prevalence there of 'absentee ownership and apparent underuse of land resources', the agency announced, the Strath of Kildonan had been 'frequently cited as a typical example of misused land'. That was why the HIDB had 'decided to examine [and report on] the strath's potential'.

Behind the scenes at the HIDB's Inverness headquarters, however, there was in fact little interest in enforcing sweeping changes in land use, whether in the Strath of Kildonan or anywhere else. It was only 'with some reluctance' and under pressure from Labour ministers, or so an HIDB staffer* wrote subsequently, that the agency's chairman, Robert Grieve, and his fellow board members went ahead with a Strath of Kildonan report which – doubtless in accordance with the steer given its authors – concluded that no case could be made 'on economic or employment grounds' for resettling the strath or otherwise interfering with the use or ownership of any of the land in or around it.

Reay Clarke was unsurprised. Prior to the HIDB embarking on its Strath of Kildonan investigations, Professor Grieve had come to Edderton Farm House to have dinner with Reay and Lydia. Next day Reay accompanied the Highland Board's chairman on a tour of the strath and was with him when, over lunch, Grieve met some of the area's owners. By that day's close, Reay knew that improved land use was not an HIDB priority – certainly not in comparison with industrial expansion of the sort Robert Grieve and his colleagues were to promote with an eagerness always absent (in the Grieve years at any rate) from HIDB consideration of anything smacking of land reform.

---

* This was James Grassie whose account of the HIDB's early years, *Highland Experiment*, was published by Aberdeen University Press in 1983.

The HIDB's embrace of heavy industry – especially its backing of a proposed petrochemical venture in which one of its board members, businessman Frank Thomson, had a substantial interest – would eventually embroil the agency in a first-order political crisis. Prior to that, however, the Highland Board had commissioned from the Jack Holmes Planning Group, a leading consultancy firm, an expensive and lavish report on how the 'Highland sub-region' extending from Inverness to Invergordon might be equipped with all manner of new towns and new enterprises. The first such enterprise to assume a definite form was an aluminium smelter to be sited on Invergordon's northern outskirts. Although early doubts as to its long-term viability were validated when, just ten years after its opening, the smelter closed with the loss of 900 jobs, the national and local support it attracted when first suggested made it unlikely that objectors to its construction would get anywhere. In his capacity as chairman of NFUS's Easter Ross Branch, however, Reay Clarke thought it right to question the smelter concept – not because he and fellow farmers opposed incoming industry on principle but because the smelter would take out of farming a thousand acres of the highest quality arable land in the Highlands. Per-acre wheat yields from that land, Reay told his Inverness Royal Academy audience at the 'Way Ahead for the Highlands' conference in December 1968, were twice the UK national average. But the smelter's arrival, he said, meant that those acres 'would never again produce food'. In an ever more populous country in an ever more populous world, that, to his mind, was wrong.

'When your rector asked me to address you,' Reay commented at that schools gathering in Inverness, 'I realised that I'd never addressed students before and that I'd better discover what you thought of this sort of conference.' For advice as to what school students would expect from him, Reay went on, he'd turned to his daughter, Janey, then sixteen. With devastating candour, she'd said simply, 'They'll come along expecting to be bored.' That was why, Reay remarked, he'd equipped himself with a large-scale map which, in the hope of retaining their interest, Reay now invited his listeners to inspect. This map, it became apparent, was Reay Clarke's riposte to the developmental strategy advocated by the HIDB and the Jack Holmes Planning Group.

A key aspect of that strategy involved a so-called 'Fast Road' between Inverness and Invergordon. This road – which the north's leading daily, the *Press and Journal*, promptly dubbed the 'Invergordon Autobahn' – was to be, for some of its length, a dual carriageway, but it was nevertheless to follow much the same route as the already existing and 150-year old main road, the A9. The Fast Road, in other words, was to reach Invergordon by skirting around, not crossing, the Beauly and Cromarty Firths. As advocated by the Jack Holmes Group and endorsed by the HIDB, this proposal was a product of a three-year-long investigative process. It was to be overturned by a map put together on the Edderton Farm House kitchen table in the course of a single Saturday evening – 'with the aid,' Reay wrote later, 'of a bottle of sherry.'

Reay shared that sherry with a longstanding friend, Aberdeen University geographer John Smith. Together, Reay recalled, he and Smith redrew the plans accompanying the Jack Holmes study: 'We moved all the Jack Holmes proposed settlements off the Class I, II and III land (the arable land) and resited them on Class IV land (areas of rough grazing and forest). When that had been done, it became obvious that the correct route for the trunk road was directly across the Beauly and Cromarty Firths.' This alternative road, Reay realised, would swallow up much less good land than the Jack Holmes option. It would shorten the journey between Inverness and Invergordon by 15 miles. And instead of stopping at Invergordon, as the Jack Holmes report recommended, the revamped A9, as envisaged by the sherry-fuelled Clarke-Smith duo, would continue north to Tain and on across the Dornoch Firth – by way of a third bridge that would cut the A9's overall length by a further 25 or so miles and, by so doing, greatly reduce travel times to East Sutherland and Caithness.

On their being put to the 200-plus sixth-year students Reay spoke with at Inverness Royal Academy on 6 December 1968, those suggestions provoked not boredom but a series of intrigued responses. Equally interested was one of the 'Way Ahead' conference's adult attendees, Tony Pledger, Highland correspondent of the *Scotsman*. Would Reay be prepared, Pledger asked, to turn his proposals into an article for his paper? This was done. Among the article's readers was Pat Hunter Gordon, managing director of Inverness's largest manufacturing company, AI Welders, and chairman of the Highland area committee of the Scottish Council Development and Industry (SCDI), a leading business lobby group. At once Pat Hunter Gordon contacted Reay with a view to lending his and the SCDI's support to the three firths crossing concept. The outcome was a cheaply produced pamphlet, written jointly by Pat Hunter Gordon, Reay Clarke and John Smith, in which the case for Beauly Firth, Cromarty Firth and Dornoch Firth bridges was set out in some detail.

The HIDB's response was scathing. Their expert consultants had thought long and hard about how best to provide the Inverness-Invergordon corridor with an up-to-date roads network, board member Prophet Smith told the press. In response, the Hunter Gordon, Clarke and Smith publication had come up with no more than a 'wiggly line' on a map. The HIDB would not be changing its mind, Smith insisted. Neither, it emerged, would Labour's Scottish Office team in Edinburgh. That, it seemed, was that.

But then, in June 1970, the Conservative Party became surprise winner of a general election. Willie Ross was replaced as Scottish Secretary by Moray and Nairn's Tory MP, Gordon Campbell, who'd heard all about the three bridges scheme from Pat Hunter Gordon. A review of Highland road options was promptly announced, and a year or so later the Beauly Firth,

Cromarty Firth and Dornoch Firth crossings, together with the necessary connecting roads, were given the go-ahead.

As always with such projects, all sorts of difficulties and delays would be encountered. But at last, on 27 August 1991, the Dornoch Bridge, a bridge Reay Clarke had first visualised 23 years before, was opened officially by Queen Elizabeth, the Queen Mother. Three weeks previously, at the invitation of its builders, Reay had driven the first car to cross its just completed carriageway. As can be seen from the prominent place given in Edderton Farm House to a photograph of that event, Reay was pleased by the communications revolution he'd done so much to bring about. Characteristically, however, the article he wrote for a celebratory supplement in the *Northern Times*, Sutherland's weekly newspaper, ended with a call to renewed action on the land use front: 'What of the future? We have built a bridge over the Dornoch Firth so that traffic can now flow freely over that stretch of water . . . As the traffic pours over the bridge, let us pause and think of the waters that flow beneath. They are waters that have come from a vast hinterland, a basin of over 400,000 acres – the parishes of Edderton, Kincardine, Lairg and Creich. They are waters that have been gathered through some 400 miles of burns and 70 miles of salmon river. If we do not take better care of the land that drains into those burns and rivers, then our countryside will continue to go back. It is land that needs cattle and oak trees. We have given it sheep and sitka spruce and too many deer. We have built bridges over the three firths. Now let us build a future for the Dornoch Firth and its great drainage basin . . . with the same sort of energy, resources and skill.'

As that 1991 article suggests, it had by then become Reay Clarke's firm view that immense and enduring ecological damage was inflicted on the Highlands by the removal from our hills and glens of the hundreds of thousands of cattle those same hills and glens supported prior to the clearances. This was an opinion reinforced when, in the mid-1970s, Reay won a Churchill Trust travel scholarship that enabled him to spend time in the Alps. 'It was a fascinating experience,' Reay wrote of his Alpine foray in a report for the Churchill Trust. 'I fell in love with this high country of Europe, its people and its farms.'

'Before the clearances,' Reay went on, 'the crofters of the north [of Scotland] practised transhumance very much as the Alpine farmer still does today. Transhumance or [as it's more commonly known in Scotland] the shieling system – the movement of stock and herders from the valley to the hill pasture in summer and back downhill again in autumn – is a system in perfect ecological balance.' In the Alps, Reay discovered, that balance had been maintained. In the Highlands, however, it had for too long been missing: 'Here at home, among the mountains and moorlands of the Scottish Highlands, we have not practised good husbandry since laird and flockmaster cleared glen and shieling of crofters and cattle to make way for "the great sheep", *na caoraich mora*.'

His having come to that conclusion meant that Reay's thinking about the Highland past was shot through with a tension evident in this book. On the one hand, Reay regretted – none more so – what had been lost to the Highlands when, during the clearances, a cattle-based agriculture gave way to one dependent on sheep. At the same time, however, Reay esteemed and respected the accomplishments of his Clarke forebears – who, as his book's account of those accomplishments underlines, were among the more prominent of the flockmasters to profit from the eradication from the Highland scene of exactly the kind of land use that so impressed Reay when he encountered it, in modern guise, in Switzerland and Austria.

Much has been written (some of it by me) about the Highland Clearances and their victims. Far less has been written about the challenges confronting the sheep farmers and shepherds whose task it was to install and then manage immense flocks of sheep on hill ground where no such flock had never before been pastured.

This book helps fill that gap. And in writing it Reay Clarke benefited greatly from the somewhat paradoxical circumstance that, despite his frequent critiques of their adverse impact on our upland ecology, Reay had himself worked closely with sheep. At Edderton the building up of a 600-strong flock of Cheviots, the breed clearance-era Gaelic-speakers knew as na caoraich mora, had been among Reay's own early ventures. Later he'd taken a job for a time as head shepherd at Ribigill, getting to grips, on that north coast sheep farm, with terrain and climate of the type his flockmaster ancestors had confronted in the course of the century or so they'd spent at nearby Eriboll – the place that features, as already indicated, more than any other in this book.

More than quarter of a century ago, on a memorable summer's day that began with an Edderton Farm House breakfast cooked by Reay's second wife Olga Matthews, Reay took me to Eriboll. As we drove the 40-mile length of single-track road that traverses inland Sutherland from Lairg by way of Altnaharra to Tongue, Reay spoke about how this now empty quarter might have looked when the people who once lived in and around it pastured their cattle on its slopes and in its corries. Years later, in June 2016, Reay returned to that same topic when I introduced him to Elizabeth Ritchie, a University of the Highlands and Islands historian with a keen interest in how livestock were managed traditionally. Reay, by this point, was in failing health and had lost much of his mobility – something he made no complaint about for all that his increasing confinement must have weighed heavily on a man accustomed to spending much of his time out of doors. He'd been reading and thinking a lot about how the typical Highland settlement of two or three centuries ago was organised, Reay told Elizabeth and me. Days afterwards, by way of an attachment to an email, he sent us the product of his researches.

'Suppose,' Reay wrote, 'we consider a Highland township of about 20 families, each with two breeding cows.' Those cows, their calves and older offspring – consisting of 100 or more beasts that might not be driven south to market until they'd reached the age of three or four – would be moved in late spring or early summer to the township's hill shielings. What Reay called 'skilled and constant herding' of the sort he'd seen in the Alps would have been required to keep cows and calves on lower and more accessible grazings while heifers and bullocks were moved ever upwards as summer greened the landscape's higher reaches.

'Their dung and urine,' Reay wrote of those cattle, 'must have made a great difference to the soil.' That soil, he went on, 'would have had a thriving population of invertebrates'. This, in turn, 'would have supported many birds' and otherwise led to greater and greater biodiversity – with, for example, 'nutrient-rich run-off' from cattle-pastured slopes helping 'to feed the trout and young salmon in the burns'. The overall result, then, 'must have been a far, far richer countryside than that which we see today'.

Might something akin to that ecologically healthier and more intensively managed, Highland countryside ever be re-established? Today when Frank Fraser Darling's 'devastated terrain' is often described and celebrated as 'wild land' – with total disregard for the fact that much of the land in question was made the way it is by human action not so very long ago – the odds against its rehabilitation and resettlement can seem insuperably high. They must have seemed all the higher to Reay Clarke in the light of officialdom's apparent lack of interest in his own modest contribution to getting people back on to the land – a contribution made possible by 2007 legislation intended to lead to the creation of 'woodland crofts'.

As the term suggests, a woodland croft is a smallholding whose occupants look to both farming and forestry for a part of their livelihoods. Just such a holding, Reay felt, could readily be laid out in a part of his own Edderton Burn Glen plantation – at a spot called Bal a'Mhuillin. 'It had been a croft long ago,' Reay commented of Bal a'Mhuillin. 'It could be a croft once again.' As soon as the relevant legislation was enacted, therefore, Reay set about making that happen – aided enthusiastically by the local couple he'd identified as his prospective holding's tenants.

'It took the three of us about nine months to get the croft registered,' Reay commented in the course of a 2012 talk he gave to one of the last land use conferences he attended. It took many more months to get other requisite permissions put in place. In all that time just one civil servant, an officer with Scotland's agricultural department, engaged constructively with Reay's Bal a'Mhuillin initiative. 'That officer was excellent,' Reay said of her. 'She was even keen to see for herself the site of our proposed croft.' But from the Crofting Commission and the Forestry Commission, the agencies ostensibly responsible for woodland croft promotion, there was, it appears, less assistance. Little was done to help him or his tenants negotiate the bureaucratic 'vale of tears' confronting them, Reay remarked – and though, when he spoke, nearly five years had elapsed since his Bal a'Mhuillin croft had taken shape, 'no-one from the Crofting Commission or the Forestry Commission [had] ever bothered to call in and see how it [was] developing.'

This depressing experience might readily have convinced a by then ageing Reay Clarke that, in the course of the half century since he and his Highland Panel colleagues urged that people be restored to places like the Strath of Kildonan, the eventual reoccupation of such places had, if anything, become less, rather than more, likely. Right to the end of his long life, however, Reay never gave up on that possibility – giving up not being in his nature. 'I am an optimist,' Reay said during one of the several public enquiries at which, in the 1960s and 1970s, he gave evidence on behalf of NFUS. 'Otherwise I wouldn't be a farmer.' They were by no means meant to be such. But as an epitaph for a comitted agriculturalist who also strove ceaselessly for Highland betterment, those words are hard to improve on.

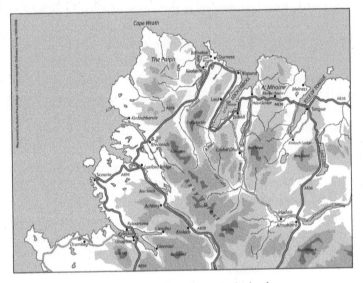

General map of north-west Sutherland.

1

Tacksmen, Clearances, Flockmasters

This is a tale set in the Reay Country, that great area of North West Sutherland which is the country of the Mackays and was once the land of their chief, Lord Reay. It is the story of my family, the Clarkes of Eriboll, who were tacksmen and then flockmasters. I tell of their way of life, of their sheep and of the land that they farmed from the late 1600s to Whitsunday 1921. I am the last of my family to have seen the working of those sheep farms. I write because the knowledge of that system of pastoral husbandry and the effect it has had on the land will be lost if it is not now recorded. It is a tale that must be told.

I feel like Miles Coverdale who, when asked by King Henry VIII to produce an English translation of the Bible, wrote: 'But to say the truth before God, it was neither my labour nor desire to have this work put in my hand . . . Therefore, when I was instantly required though I could not do it as well as I would, I thought it my duty to do my best, and that with a good will.'[1]

My book deals with the two hundred year period between the start of the eighteenth century and the opening decades of the twentieth. The first part of that period witnessed the destruction of the clan society and the ending of the traditional role of the tacksman who had been a key element of that society. The clearances followed when the people were removed from their land to make room for the flockmasters and their sheep. These flockmasters developed a system of pastoral husbandry that was to become standard practice on the hills and moors of Sutherland. The final hundred years of that period also witnessed a dramatic

1   Professor William Barclay, *Through the Year with William Barclay*, 1971.

fall in the fertility of the soil of that land and a whittling away of the natural wealth of that countryside.

The story starts with the records that we have of Clarkes farming around Tongue, it follows with one John Clarke (*c.* 1680–*c.* 1730), tacksman of Glendhu, and continues on firmer ground with his son, James Clarke (1703–1774). James was the tacksman, first of the farm of Cnocbreack and then of Clashneach, both farms being in the parish of Durness. The tale continues through the clearances with James' sons thereby acquiring the tenancies of several good farms. There follows the saga of the fortunes of the Clarke family as flockmasters at Eriboll. The story ends with the Board of Agriculture taking over the tenancy of that farm from the Clarkes in 1921. It is a tale of tacksmen and of clearances and of flockmasters.

Tacksmen

Under the old traditional system of farming, the tack or tenancy of a farm was granted to a tacksman by the chief of the clan. The tacksmen were answerable to the chief and formed the middle class of that society. They were the local leaders. Originally the tacksman, often a relative of the chief, was required to supply a number of fighting men from his tack when there was a call to arms. The tacksman also had to give the chief a proportion of the annual produce of that tack and a small cash rent. The tacksman gathered subtenants who built their houses on the tack and were granted the use of the arable land to grow their crops. They also kept their cattle there for much of the year but in summer herded them collectively on the high ground, on the shielings. In return, the subtenants were required to hand over to the tacksman a large proportion of the crops and of the produce, such as butter and cheese. Further, the subtenants provided services such as herding the tacksman's cattle, cutting and carting his peats and much else. The arable lands were not fenced and so, in early summer to protect the growing crops, the cattle and other stock were moved up to the shielings. There the wives and young folk herded the cattle and made butter and cheese. In the autumn when the crops had been harvested, all descended again to the arable lands on the floor of the glen.

The high pastures were then rested until spring came round once more. It was a transhumant system. It built fertility and created productive swards on the hill pastures. However the weakness of the system lay in the husbandry of the in-bye land. Here the cropping of the land was laid out in strips or rigs – hence run rigs. Which subtenant cropped which rig was determined by lot each spring under the supervision of the tacksman. Each rig was cropped by the same subtenant for only one year. He was most unlikely to get that rig again. It was the luck of the draw. There was therefore no incentive for any subtenant to carry out any improvement on that or on any other rig.

Clearances

During the late 1700s the population increased. The husbandry of the arable land did not improve and so the yield of food from that land did not increase. The resultant hunger, particularly after difficult seasons, caused interest to be aroused in systems of husbandry different from that which had been practised for long by the tacksman and his subtenants. With the coming of peace after the rebellion in 1745, the clan chiefs were seeking rents that would support their new lifestyle. They wanted cash from their land rather than butter, cheese and services. The opportunity to rent out land to sheep farmers for large cash rents was therefore most appealing. Earlier Lord Reay had brought a flock of sheep up from the south – from the Borders with Border shepherds to herd them – and settled them on the Parph, that great stretch of land lying inland from Cape Wrath and west of the Kyle of Durness. These Southern sheep were much bigger and produced a heavier fleece than the native sheep. These were the Great Sheep, *an Caorach Mhor*. The small native sheep, *Seana chaoirich beaga*, – and they were few in number – had been treated almost as pets, in-wintered and kept largely for their milk, which was made into cheese. The extreme difference between the care of the native sheep and the extensive husbandry of these new sheep from the Borders must have been a source of wonder and of great interest.

To the natives of the north the keeping of a vast flock of sheep, out-of-doors, all the year round and herding them with collie dogs must have seemed quite extraordinary. Yet clearly these new sheep were thriving well on the clean pastures of the Parph – clean from having previously been grazed in summer almost solely by cattle. The possibility of keeping large flocks of these sheep on the extensive hills of Sutherland to produce a heavy wool clip and big joints of mutton attracted the attention of flockmasters from the south. They were prepared to pay large cash rents and this appealed greatly to the land owners. However the problem with this new system was what was to be done with the native population that had occupied these lands since time immemorial. The answer was 'The Clearances' – clear the people from their homes in the glens and move them down to the coast or ship them overseas to the colonies of the British Empire. Potential large sheep farms, cleared of troublesome natives, would then be available for letting to enterprising flockmasters, willing to pay large cash rents. The hardships suffered by the natives have been well recognised both in oral tradition and in literature but the land suffered too. The damage done to the environment by the abandonment of the transhumant system has not been widely recorded.

Flockmasters

The flockmasters, who established the sheep industry in Sutherland, were mainly from beyond the Highlands, but there were a few who had been born in the North and who saw great opportunities in this new system. Flockmasters had to be able to raise the necessary capital to take a lease of one of the new sheep farms and to stock it. A number seem to have come from Argyll where 'the big sheep' had been introduced somewhat earlier. The most notable flockmaster in Sutherland of those early days was Patrick Sellar from Moray, who had trained in law and who became a factor for the Sutherland Estate. He cleared Strathnaver (and elsewhere), and created there one of the most successful sheep farms. He stocked it with Cheviot sheep and staffed it with shepherds from the Borders.

The flockmaster of those early days was a man of energy and enterprise and a hard man. He had to be, otherwise he would not succeed. The task of getting sheep settled on new ground was a difficult one for such sheep would wish to wander off far across the unfenced hills of Sutherland. Even when the ewes had been herded well for months on end, come lambing time the urge to get back to their original home was stronger than ever. The shepherd had to be out on the hill at all times and in all weathers keeping them in on their own ground, and the flockmaster saw to it that he did just that.

There were bad times and there were good times. The end of the Napoleonic war brought a serious fall in the price of wool and mutton. A number of flockmasters went bankrupt. Those that survived went on to experience several decades of great prosperity and to enjoy an enviable lifestyle. The Duke of Sutherland was by then the owner of almost the whole of Sutherland. He had fine farmhouses built for his flockmasters. Domestic staff – cooks and housemaids and nursemaids – were readily available to tend to all the needs of the household. The landowners were the upper class but the flockmasters were the real leaders of that society. They were respected for their skill – they knew their sheep – and for their growing wealth and position.

The flockmasters possessed large flocks of sheep and were farming on a big scale, maybe the largest farming enterprises in Britain at that time, both in terms of acreages farmed and in numbers of sheep owned. 4,269 sheep plus lambs are listed in the 1833 Eriboll clipping count. 7,232 sheep plus lambs are recorded in the valuation of the stock on Melness in 1890 and that farm then extended to over 70,000 acres. In the 1881 census George Granville Clarke is listed as farming 40,000 acres of hill pasture plus 800 acres of arable and employing 40 men and up to 30 women. 5,118 sheep plus lambs are recorded in the valuation of the Eriboll sheep stock in 1921. These were large farming enterprises that the flockmasters established, and they handled them very successfully.

2
John Clark of Glendhu (c. 1680–c. 1730)

John Clark of Glendhu – John Clark of the Dark Glen – is the first Clark in the direct line of our family of whom we have any record and even that is very slight. His name appears on an old family tree. He must have lived in the closing years of the seventeenth century. It is likely that he was born around 1680 and died perhaps some fifty years later, possibly about 1730. I am only guessing. We don't really know when he lived, whom he married, or how many children they had. He certainly had a son, called James, born in 1705, and we have firm evidence of James. However we know where John lived and that was at Glendhu, for the record refers to him as 'John Clark of Glendhu'. There are two glens by the name of Glen Dhu (the Dark Glen) in north-west Sutherland. One is Glendhu in the parish of Eddrachillis, on the north side of the sea loch, Loch Glendhu. Loch Glendhu can be seen today looking east from the Kylesku Bridge. It was a great loch for the herring; 'There has not only been a greater quantity of fish killed on the coast of this parish [Eddrachillis] for some years past, than on the coast of any other place in the Highlands, but more herring than what have been killed on all the coasts of all the Highlands put together', writes Rev Mr Alexander Falconer, minister of that parish, in the *First Statistical Account* in 1790.[2] The Rev Alexander Falconer had a daughter, who was destined to marry a grandson of John Clark and live at Eriboll.

The other Glendu (sic) is in Assynt, the neighbouring parish on the south side of that long sea inlet made up of Loch Cairnbawn, Loch Glendhu and Loch Glencoul. This Glendu is listed along with Culack and Camore as oxgates of the farm of Kirktown,

2   Sir John Sinclair, *First Statistical Account*, 1791.

which is near Inchnadamph. John Home's *Survey of Assynt* in 1774 states: '. . . to the head of Glendu at the East, the pasture is remarkably fertile abounding with the finest sweet grass.'[3]

I am not certain which of these two dark glens was the home of John Clark, but I think it must have been Glendhu in the parish of Eddrachillis. Eddrachillis is in the Mackay country, in those days part of the lands of Lord Reay. The Clarks had a long association with Lord Reay, chief of Clan Mackay. The Parish of Assynt to the south belonged to the Countess of Sutherland. If I am right and John Clark was of Glendhu in the parish of Eddrachillis, then his grandson, Charles Clarke, would move there in 1801 as tenant of his grandfather's very farm. Charles would later farm much of the surrounding land as well. His son, James, was to emigrate to Tasmania and there create another Glendhu, a farm which still exists today. Of all that, I will tell later.

Clark(e) – The Early Records

The name 'Clarke' or 'Clark' (with or without the 'e' – they were all the same family) and their connection with Tongue appear in the National Records of Scotland as far back as the 1600s. Indeed there have long been families of Clark(e)s living in the north of Sutherland. How long the Clark family has actually lived in the north or where they had come from or why they came to settle in the Mackay country is not yet known. Nor is it certain that the Clark(e)s, who are listed here and who farmed around Tongue are the same Clarkes as my family. All that I can say is that, within the family, it has always been accepted that these were the same Clarkes. There is also an oral tradition that they originally came from Yorkshire but when or why remains to be discovered. The name for a clerk in Gaelic is *cleireach* and means a person having literacy and learning. This ability to write was present in the Clarke family. In those days most of the people in the Highlands

3   R.J. Adam (Editor), *John Home's Survey of Assynt*, 1960.

were unable to write their names and would have made a cross or mark when acting as a witness to a document. However the Clarkes, when acting as witnesses, always wrote their names on documents recorded in the Reay papers. From the 1600s onwards, the name Clark appears many times in the Reay papers, usually as a witness or witnesses to legal documents such as tacks (a form of lease) or bonds.

In May 1615, Mr Alexander Clark, a notary public, acts as a witness for a tack (lease) granted by Alexander, Bishop of Caithness, to Donald Mackay, Fiar (Feuer?) of Strathnaver. Then in May 1637, Alexander Clark 'in Tung' (Tongue) acts as a witness to Bonds signed by Donald, 1st Lord Reay, and, again in October of that year, Alexander acts as witness to another Bond granted by Lord Reay. Then in February 1644 Alexander Clark – this time styled 'Baillie Alexander Clark in Langwell' – acts as witness to an Instrument of Sasine relating to the alienation of land at Skerray and Ribigill. The principle signatory to this document is John, Master of Reay. This John, Master of Reay, became the 2nd Lord Reay on the death of his father in 1649. In December 1663 Hector Clark in Strathmelness acts as witness to the granting of a tack by John, now Lord Reay. Then in 1676, Donald Clark and Murdo Clark act as witnesses to a wadset between John, Lord Reay and Angus Mackay of Melness. The places where these deeds were signed are either Tongue ('Tung', 'Townge' or 'Tong') or at Balnakiel near Durness. At each of these places Lord Reay had had built and later would rebuild 'A Big House' – *Tigh Mor* – and these houses were the official residences of the chiefs of the Clan Mackay, the Lords Reay.

And so the name Clark frequently appears on the rent rolls[4] of the lands of Lord Reay. It would appear that, particularly around the Kyle of Tongue, there were a number of Clark families settled and farming. In March 1678, Alexander Clark and Angus Clark are listed among the tacksmen at Skail, as are four Clarks – Angus

4   Angus Mackay, *The Book of Mackay*, 1906.

Clark, Donald Clark, Donald Beg Clark, and William Clark –
listed as tacksmen at Kenloch (Kinloch at the head of the Kyle of
Tongue). Then later in 1789, the rent rolls show Alexander Clark
paying rent for Strathtongue and Peter Clark for Kinlochmore,
both farms in the parish of Tongue. James Clarke's widow appears
as tenant of Clashneach in Durness. Robert Clark is listed as
tacksman of Un Stephan and Borscaig. Un Stephan and Borscaig
are both on the west side of the Kyle of Tongue, across the water
from Castle Varrich, and may have been somewhere near the
ferryman's house. This was built by the Duke of Sutherland in
the days of the ferry across the Kyle of Tongue and was complete
with stabling for travellers' horses.

It does appear that down the years the Clark family was well
known to the chiefs of Clan Mackay and trusted by them. From
the rent rolls it would also appear that it was the bigger and better
farms of which the Clarks were the tenants. There is little point
in being on friendly terms with the clan chief if you can't get the
lease of a really good farm for yourself or for your son or sons.

3

The Clarkes and the Reay Fencibles

One of the sons of Robert Clark, tacksman of Un Stephan and Borscaig, was Piper George Clarke (c. 1774–*c.* 1824), who joined the Reay Fencibles when that regiment was raised at Tongue in 1794. This was a stirring event in the Reay Country. It is told that Reisimeid Mhic Aoidh, the widow of Angus, the son of John, went to Bighouse from Strathmore below Ben Hope with her seven sons in answer to this call to arms by their clan chief, Lord Reay. These sons were all tall, stout, powerful fellows, the smallest being over six feet in height. The sight of so stalwart a family excited the admiration and curiosity of Colonel Mackay of Bighouse, who had been appointed to command the Reay Fencibles. He enquired of the widow, '*Gu de air an d'araich thu na gillean?*' ('On what did you rear the lads?') to which she replied, '*Dh'araich, Bhiogais, le 'r cead, air im is cais, is feol an fheidh is iasg a' bhradain, agus aran cruaidh coric' a' bhrathainn!*' ('By your leave, Bighouse, I reared them on butter and cheese, the flesh of the deer, the salmon and the hard oatcakes of the quern.') Bighouse gave the widow permission to take her favourite son back with her. She selected the youngest; on being asked why she chose him, replied: '*Do bhrigh gur esan is oige, agus gur e is miosa a bheir 'n-aire air e fhein!*' ('Because he, being the youngest, is the least able to take care of himself!')[5]

Some 800 men joined this new regiment in the course of a few weeks. 'That pipe music was fostered in the Reay Fencibles there can be no doubt, and indeed it would be strange if it had been otherwise for the Mackay Country was noted for the excellence of its pipers . . .' 'At that time' writes the author of *The Highland Bagpipe*, 'there were more pipers from the Reay Country in the

5   I. H. Mackay Scobie, *An Old Highland Fencible Corps*, Edinburgh 1914.

11

army than from any other district in Scotland. Skye and Tongue produced more pipers and gave more pipers to the army than any other two districts.'[6] The Reay Fencibles were recruited only for military duties within Great Britain and Ireland. They were sent to Ireland in 1795 and served with distinction in that country, particularly at the Battle of Tara Hill. The regiment returned to Scotland and was disbanded in 1802.

Two Clarkes from Durness joined, both being sons of James Clarke (1705–1774), tacksman of Clashneach, of whom more shall be told later. One was his second son, Alexander (1760–1822) who is listed as the captain lieutenant in 1796 and, as such, commanded the Colonel's company. He was also the Paymaster to the Regiment and six years later (1802) was a full captain when the Reay Fencibles were disbanded. He was then appointed as a lieutenant of marines on half pay; he was later a captain in the Sutherland Volunteers. The other was James' sixth son, Hugh (1766–1807). He is listed as a lieutenant but resigned on 30th June 1797 after three years' service.[7]

However it was another Clarke, the aforementioned Piper George Clarke, who was destined to have the more distinguished military career. We cannot be certain that he was of our family but his portrait, of which I tell later, has been long in the family and has been handed down to me for safe-keeping. Piper George Clarke was born in Tongue, was a piper and enlisted there as such in the Reay Fencibles on 27th June 1794. When the Reay Fencibles returned from Ireland, Piper George Clarke transferred to the Regular Army, to the 71st Highland Regiment, which regiment later became the Highland Light Infantry. The Regular Army was keen to recruit trained soldiers from the Fencible Regiments and offered a considerable bounty to any who did transfer.

Piper George Clarke then went with the 71st Highland Regiment under Wellington to the Peninsular War in Portugal and

6   W. L. Manson, *The Highland Bagpipe*, Harvard 1901.
7   I. H. Mackay Scobie, *An Old Highland Fencible Corps*, Edinburgh 1914.

Spain and saw much active service there. At the Battle of Vimeiro in Portugal on 21st August 1808, when Wellington defeated the French forces under General Junot, Piper George Clarke was badly wounded in the groin during a charge on the French position. He was unable to stand but continued to play his pipes sitting down. He so cheered his companions with his playing of 'Up and waur them a', Willie' that they 'hurled the French into confusion and re-took the guns'. Eventually, he was exhausted by loss of blood and 'handed over his pipes to a bystander with strict instructions to take them to his commanding officer'. In 1813 Piper George Clarke was again wounded at the battle of Vittoria in Spain, this time in the left leg and arm.

In January 1816 he was honourably discharged from the army. His Discharge Certificate reads, '. . . but in consequence of being worn out and severe wounded is rendered unfit for further service and is hereby discharged'. It also states that he was then forty-two years of age, five feet nine inches in height, with dark brown hair, grey eyes, a fair complexion and, by trade, a labourer. He could write, for he has personally signed his Discharge Certificate. This is unusual. 80% of those discharged at that time put an X against their signatures as they could not write. He had served five years and twelve days as a private with the Reay Fencibles; then eight years and forty-four days as a private plus seven years and thirty-three days as a sergeant with the 71st Regiment, making a total of twenty-one years and 189 days service. Major George Spottiswoode, commanding 2nd Battalion, 71st Regiment of Light Infantry, has added a notable personal commendation to the bottom of the Discharge Certificate:[8]

Given under my Hand and Seal of the Regiment at *Glasgow* the *eighth* day of *December 1815.*

The above mentioned Sergeant George Clark was made sergeant at the request of Lt General Sir Ronald Crawford

8   *The Highland Light Infantry Chronicle,* January 1931.

Ferguson on the 27th August 1808 for remarkably gallant conduct as piper of the Regt. at the Battle of Vimeira altho' he could not be borne on the strength <u>as Sergt.</u> for some time after owing to the want of a vacancy. He was wounded at Vimeira in the groin and at Vittoria in the left leg and arm.

George Spottiswoode Major
Commanding 2 Bn 71st. Lt Infy

And that was not all. Later in 1816, the Highland Society of London presented him with a gold medal and a silver-mounted set of bagpipes upon which was engraved:

To George Clarke, piper of the 71st, as a mark of the Society's approbation of his spirited and laudable conduct at the Battle of Vimeira, Augst. 21st 1808, in continuing to play upon his pipes to animate the men after being himself severely wounded.

He was also presented with his portrait by the Society, who had commissioned Franz Manskirch to paint him in the full Highland dress of an army piper.[9]

It is very probable that he spent the last years of his life at Fort George, near Inverness, as an army pensioner. He was a noted and much respected old soldier and was called 'The Piper of Vimeira'. He died in about 1825, then aged about fifty years old. It is on record that: 'At his death a monument was erected over his grave at Fort George by his regiment' (*An Old Highland Fencible Corps*, Capt I. H. Mackay Scobie, 1914). At present no trace of that monument can be found at Fort George.[10]

---

9 Diana M Henderson *The Scottish Regiments*.

10 I. H. Mackay Scobie *An Old Highland Fencible Corps*, Edinburgh 1914.

4
James Clarke (1705–1774)

Tacksman of Cnocbreac and then of Clashneach, Durness. Died 30 March 1774, aged sixty-nine years. Ground Officer of Durness for Lord Reay. Married Margaret Mackay (1726–1805), grand-daughter of Charles, son of Donald, first Lord Reay. Died 29 September 1805, aged seventy-nine years.

Children

There were nine children, seven boys and two girls; all born in the space of eighteen years.

Barbara (*c.* 1752–?), married Robert Mackay.

George (1754–1780), Lieutenant, Honourable East India Company. He was killed in action in India, serving under Sir Hector Munro.

Donald (1756–?), went out to Jamaica and died in West Indies.

Robert (1759–?), went out to Jamaica and died in West Indies.

Alexander (1760–1822), Oldnay. Captain, the Reay Fencibles. Also one time tacksman of Culkine. Died at Eriboll on 20 June 1822. Married Johan Mackay, daughter of Captain John Mackay, Oldnay; 31st Foot.

Hugh (1765–1842), Lieutenant, The Reay Fencibles. Died aged seventy-seven years. Tacksman of Culkein and of Oldnay. Married Janet Mackay, daughter of Captain John Mackay, Oldnay; 31st Foot.

Charles* (1767–*c.* 1831), Flockmaster, Glen Dhu, Glen Coul

* Each asterisked name is the subject of a chapter in this book.

and elsewhere. Married Alexina Scobie, Ardvar. Died 3 June 1831 aged sixty-four. [Father of James* (1791–1853) who emigrated to Tasmania and there established the farm of Glen Dhu on the River Ouse.]

Mary (1768–?), spouse unknown; twelve children.

John* (1770–1837) Flockmaster at Keoldale and then at Eriboll. Married Johanna Falconer (1774–1858), daughter of Rev. Alexander Falconer, Eddrachillis.

The only child of John Clark of Glendhu for whom we have any written record or indeed any firm knowledge is James Clarke (1705–1774). He was the tacksman, first of Cnocbreack and then of Clashneach, both in the parish of Durness. He married Margaret Mackay (1726–1805). She was a grand-daughter of Charles Mackay who was the son of Donald, first Lord Reay. It looks as though the Clarke family's past connections and good standing with Lord Reay were most useful and were further strengthened by this marriage. However that may be and notwithstanding that Margaret was twenty-one years younger than her husband, their marriage has the hallmarks of a happy marriage. She bore him nine children – seven boys and two girls. They were a successful farming family, first at the farm of Cnocbreack which lies near the main road about a mile south of the present village of Durness. On the 1790 map it is marked as lying within the corn lands of Durness and not far from the school and the manse. In 1767 – he was then sixty-two – he took the tack of the farm of Clashneach, a bigger and better farm, on the west side of Loch Borralie and a mile to the west of Cnocbreack. It is possible that he may then have farmed both farms. At the time he took the tack of Clashneach, their family was still young. Of that family of nine children, George, the oldest was then eleven years old and Charles, at that time the youngest, was born in that year. The last child to be born was John and he arrived three years later in 1770 when Margaret was forty-four and her husband sixty-seven. There was quite a family for Margaret to look after. George (1756–1822) was the eldest who served under General Sir Hector Munro as a lieutenant in the army with the East India Company. He was killed in action out there in 1780 at the age of twenty-four. Of Barbara, the eldest daughter, we don't know anything at all. Their third child, Alexander (1760–1822), joined the Reay Fencible Regiment, which was raised by Lord Reay at Tongue in 1794. Alexander is listed on the Regiment's strength in 1796 as the Captain-Lieutenant and, as such, commanded the Colonel's company. He was a full captain six years later (1802) when they were disbanded and he was then appointed as a Lieutenant of Marines on half pay. He was afterwards a Captain in the Sutherland Volunteers. He married Johan Mackay of Oldnay. He died at Eriboll in 1822.

The next two were Donald (c. 1762–?) and Robert (c. 1763–?). Both were born in the early 1760s, both went out to the West Indies to seek their fortune and both died out there while still young. The toll of death from disease in that part of the world at that time was serious. When Mr Graham Bruce, the former schoolmaster at Durness, excavated the remains of the farmhouse at Clashneach he found a number of artefacts such as buttons and pottery which came from the West Indies. We will never know whether the boys sent these home as presents for their mother or were able to come home on leave and hand them to her; probably the former.

Then there was Hugh (1765–1807). He farmed in Sutherland, in the parish of Assynt. We don't know whom he married but we do know that they had five of a family. He died young, at the age of forty-two years. By that time he was tacksman of Culkein, Drumbeg in Assynt and also farmed Oldnay. These were large farms, some four thousand acres in all of which about a hundred acres were arable. His widow stayed on after his death and she made a home there for Charles, his brother, after he had become bankrupt in 1824. Both Hugh and Charles are buried at Scourie.

Of Charles* (1767–1830), we know much more. He became tenant of Glendhu, almost certainly the same Glendhu as the farm where his grandfather, John Clark, had been tacksman. Charles married Alexina Scobie of Ardvar, another large Assynt farm of almost two thousand acres of which about fifty were arable. Charles looks to have been a capable farmer and flockmaster. He was also involved in fishing as a merchant. He expanded his farming from Glendhu and Glenbeg to become tenant of several surrounding farms. Then prices crashed and he was declared bankrupt in 1824. He will get a chapter to himself later.

There is no record of Mary's (c. 1769–?) life or husband apart from the fact that they had a family of twelve children; six boys and six girls. And finally John* (1770–1837), who started farming at Keoldale, of which farm Clashneach is now a part, in 1802. He married Johanna Falconer (1774–1858) and they had eleven children – six boys and five girls. In 1815, he exchanged the tenancy of Keoldale for the tenancy of Eriboll, while the Scobies, who had been tenants of Eriboll, moved to Keoldale. Why this exchange took place we will probably never know although it may have been over the matter of rent. Of all James' children, John was probably the most successful farmer. The eldest of John's children, Alexander, was to become one of the great flockmasters of Sutherland as was his son, George Granville. These two deserve and will be given chapters to themselves.

So James Clark was the tacksman of Clashneach. The tacksmen were the middle class of that society and as such were the leading figures on the estate. They were next to the chief in seniority and in the days of inter-clan warfare had served as the leaders in the raiding parties. Later they served as officers in the army. They were the platoon and company commanders. In earlier times they were required to supply their chief with a number of fighting men as part of the agreement for their holding of a tack. The tacksman's land was worked and his stock was herded by his subtenants who lived on the farm. They paid a rent and were granted the keep of a small number of cows and their followers. Below these small tenants were the cottars who had a house and scarce any other privileges. They picked a living as best they could. The whole farm was like a large untidy family, in theory all helping each other. In practice, being human, there were many levels of mutual help and many levels of the lack of it. Some tacksmen cared for their people and many did not. With more settled times and the introduction of somewhat better medical attention in the late eighteenth century the population started to increase. Under the system of run-rig and share farming, the arable land failed to produce sufficient to feed this growing population. Indeed the Reay Country had never been able to produce enough grain during the historical period.

As well as farming, James was appointed ground officer for the parish of Durness by Lord Reay. The ground officer was the under factor for the parish and it was a post with authority and influence. He would have had to settle disputes between the other tacksmen and their small tenants and to arbitrate on disagreements about the boundaries of the inbye land and the shielings. The position of ground officer would also have given him some say in the selection of tenants for any farm which fell vacant and in other matters.

The Manner of the Husbandry

With the run-rig system the different rigs were regularly re-allocated to the subtenants of the tacksman by casting lots as to who would be allocated each rig for cropping. They then set to and ploughed, manured and sowed their crops on the rigs so allotted. In the autumn after the crops had been harvested, the cattle would come down from the shielings and all the arable land would be thrown open to them. Each cattle beast was owned by an individual subtenant and the tacksman himself also owned a number of the cattle. Even the cottars, who only had a cottage and no right to a rig, often possessed a cow of their own. Yet all the herding was done jointly. Most of the cattle would spend the winter on the rigs, grazing the grass and weeds on the baulks between these rigs, eked out with straw and maybe some hay. Some of the cows would be in-wintered inside the houses. It was most unlikely that any subtenant would continue to get the same rig to crop for a number of years running and herein was the great weakness of the run-rig system. There was no incentive to do anything to improve a rig when you knew that you were most unlikely to get that particular rig to crop again.

The run-rigs varied in size but were usually about five to six yards wide and as long as fitted the terrain. They were ploughed on a slight curve to ease the turning of the plough at the endrig. They were ploughed as a gathering, up one side and down the other, always in the same direction. Some were dug with the spade. They were fertilised with the dung from the winter, both animal and human, seaweed gathered from the shore and the old thatch whenever a house got a new thatched roof of heather or straw or bracken. Over the years the rigs became higher in the centre, rounded in cross section, and with a hollow between each one. These hollows between each rig formed a primitive drain and grew a great mass of weeds that seeded out into the growing crop. To a visitor from the south these fields of rigs must have looked to be an untidy and ill-ordered system of farming. The low rounded strips of ploughing alternated with unploughed damp hollows, which grew only a mass of weeds, and all were scattered across the township without any regular form or pattern.

All the farmes ill disposed and mixed, different persons having alternate ridges; not one wheel carriage on the estate. Nor indeed any one road that would allow it . . .

the whole land raised and uneven, and full of stones . . . and all the ridges crooked in the shape of an S, and very high, full of noxious weeds and poor, being worn out by culture, without proper manure and tillage.[11]

Thus wrote Sir Archibald Grant of Monymusk describing the condition of his estate in Aberdeenshire in the middle of the eighteenth century and before his zeal for 'improvements' had started to transform that countryside. The farmland around Durness probably looked also something like this in the late 1700s and early 1800s.

Under this system of husbandry, the crops that were grown were bere, a form of barley notable for being able to grow in acid soils, and oats. These provided the cereal item of diet for the human population; some of the bere was used for the making of the whisky. Potatoes started to be grown in the mid-eighteenth century and maybe some turnips perhaps fifty years later. The crops were poor and gave very low yields. Indeed they were terribly poor by today's standards but they did supply a hardy, virile population with their needs for the cereal part of their diet for part of the year. The people must have been very hungry in the years of bad harvests and meal was often imported. Bad harvests seem to have occurred about every ten years or so. The Rev Mr William Mackenzie, minister of the parish of Assynt, writing in *First Statistical Account* (printed in 1795) states:

In the spring of 1772, in consequence of the preceeding indifferent harvest, one-fourth part of the cattle perished . . . In short, by observation, the narrator can truly say that every 9th or 10th year turns out distressing, either by loss of crop, loss of cattle, perhaps both if the spring proves not favourable; and in the same proportion of years presently mentioned, there is generally a failure of credit

11 J. Stuart (Editor), *Monymusk Papers.*

by drovers in more or less degree; for, as they drive all the cattle sold here, and other neighbouring parishes, to the southern markets, they must necessarily feel the effects of bad seasons and times; and such is the case here at present. The intermediate years betwixt every 9th or 10th year, are, upon the whole, not to be complained of.[12]

I am sure that the people were indeed thankful for 'those intermediate years'. It must be borne in mind that there are no records of actual starvation during those times. Starvation was to come in the next century during the potato famine when potato blight appeared and virtually destroyed the crop.

James' wife, Margaret Clarke, clearly believed that there was no point in being a relative of the chief if you couldn't get tenancies of farms – and good farms – for your sons. When the time came, at least two of her boys were granted the tenancies of desirable farms. John got the tenancy of Keoldale in 1802 and Charles got the tenancy of Glen Dhu and Glen Coul in 1818. Perhaps her hand was also behind Hugh getting the tenancy of Culkein, Drumbeg and Thomas, John's nephew, later getting the tenancy of Stronrubie, although both these farms are in the parish of Assynt, which was then owned by the Countess of Sutherland. They were both good farms. Much earlier the surveyor, John Home, in his survey of Assynt in 1774, had listed Culkein as being of nine hundred acres, of which forty-nine were infield, and Inchnadamph as being of 3,174 acres, of which seventy-five were infield. Of Inchnadamph he writes: '. . . the haughs along the Burn from Loch Ha are pretty dry yielding good Corn and when in grass make rich Meadow-Ground'.[13]

James held the tacks of Cnocbreak and Clashneach, both farms being part of the 'Corn Lands of Durness'. They are shown laid out in rigs on the map of 1790. Both these farms would also have had

12 Sir John Sinclair, *First Statistical Account*, 1791.
13 R. J. Adam (Editor), *John Home's Survey of Assynt*, Edinburgh 1960.

the right to graze certain shielings in the hills. The land was worked in a system of husbandry that combined the growing of crop on the arable lands with the transhumant practice of summering the cattle and all the other livestock up in the hills. The arable lands (the inbye) was separated from the outrun (the outbye) by a head dyke, built of drystone or turf or a combination of both. Inside the head dyke on the inbye were the dwelling houses, the rigs and much waste land, which was uncropped because it was wet or rocky. Beyond the head dyke was the higher, poorer land (the outbye). The better parts of this might, now and then, be cut for hay but in the main this was grazing land. Turf was cut here for such uses as the repair of the head dyke and as a base for the thatching of the roofs. Further out and higher up on the hill were the shielings with stone or turf huts for the seasonal use of those who herded the stock there during the summer months.

In James Clarke's time cattle were the keystone. They were the wealth of the people and were recognised as such. These cattle were small, hardy and late maturing. The cows would not carry a calf every year and there were losses. Indeed the Highland cattle breed have had the reputation of being shy breeders although this may now be undeserved. However there were plenty of cattle beasts, for the stirks were kept until four years old before setting off for sale at the great trysts in the south of Scotland. This meant that for every cow there could be at times five followers – her calf of that year plus her one, two, three and four year old descendants, provided they had all survived and that was by no means certain. In late spring or early summer all these cattle plus the bulls, the sheep, the goats and the ponies left the township on their annual journeying up to the high shielings. The women also went to herd the cows and to milk them and to turn that milk into butter and cheese. In the long days of summer the pastures of those mountain shielings provided the butter and cheese that would feed the family in the winter and also provided a portion of the rent which the tacksman had to pay the clan chief. The higher and poorer grazings provided the keep for the rearing of the eild stock and the ponies. Ecologically it was beautiful. It followed the age-old rules of wise pasture management, being grazed mainly by cattle in the growing season, with a few sheep and goats to keep the perennial weeds under control.

It was then left to rest, completely ungrazed from autumn until the following late spring. There were scarce any deer to disturb this rest. One account estimates that there were only about 1,500 deer in the whole of Sutherland at that time.[14] A number of these would have been in the Reay Forest. After the stock had returned to the low ground, the grasses, clovers and herbs continued to grow and nutrients were stored in the leaves and the roots. When spring came round once more, these started off the growth as temperatures rose. The pastures profited greatly from that essential period of complete rest. In the spring the cattle only returned to the shielings when each plant had established enough leaf to start photosynthesis. This was brought on by the return of longer daylight and warmer days. In almost all townships a grass keeper was appointed to see that the age old rules of pastoral husbandry were observed. At the first signs of growth in the grass, the grass keeper would start going up to the mountains to ensure that the neighbours did not try to slip their stock on to the pastures and steal the early bite. When he considered that there was enough growth of grass and only then would the township gather up their equipment and bedding and drive the stock up to the shieling. The older cows would remember the way and would lead the procession. Grass was sweet up in the mountains and all – women and children and young men and maidens – would look forward to those days in the hills. This was the happy time. There were no sheep in the meadow, nor cows in the corn. The hunger and cold of the winter were over. Long warm days lay ahead with

14 William Scrope, *Days of Deer-stalking in the Scottish Highlands*, 1883.

full bellies for the stock. No wonder that the Gaelic songs of the shielings tell of laughter and love. The shieling huts were built near a burn or a spring. A trace of the one-time wealth of those pastures, established by this pattern of seasonal grazing, can still be seen today in the scattered green or bracken-covered patches on hillsides of heather and deer grass.

In the east of the parish of Durness were the mountain pastures of Beinn Ceannabeinne, Meall Meadhonach and Ben Spionnaidh where the cattle would go to spend these long days of summer. Some may have summered across the Kyle of Durness. There on the Parph are place names such as *Buaile* (cattle fold), *Loch Airaidh* (Loch of the Shieling) and *Cnoc na Ba Ruaidhe* (Hill of the Red Cattle). On the present Ordnance Survey map there is a site marked as 'Old Shielings'. There must have been many more of these telling names and now they are lost. Those which we still have tell us how these lands were worked before the coming of the great sheep.

The pastoral farming of transhumance was the movement of the stock, cattle with some sheep, goats and ponies, going up to the hill pastures, the shielings, for the summer months and returning in the autumn to the arable – the inbye land – once the crops had been ingathered. There on the inbye they spent the winter, grazing the residues of the crops, the weeds and grasses, supplemented with straw and some hay.

This system of transhumance is no longer practised in the Highlands of Scotland but still continues in mountainous country throughout the world. Particularly in the Alps, cattle are driven up to the high pastures, the Hoch Alm, in early summer where their milk is turned into butter and cheese. It is a beautifully balanced system which creates a countryside of flowered meadows, rich in wildlife. Long ago in the Highlands, cereals from the inbye and dairy products from the hill, with berries and nuts and fish – supplemented maybe with some salmon and venison if the opportunity presented itself – raised a hardy race. All this was going to be destroyed by the economic pressures that lay ahead. The short term principles of economics take preference over the long term needs of the land.

James lived through times of great change. In his youth the system of chief, tacksmen, subtenants and cottars determined the social order and farmed the land. This began to alter when James was in his forties. Following the defeat of the Jacobite forces at Culloden in 1746, the government was determined to end the power of the chiefs and to establish recognised law and order throughout the Highlands. Durness and the Reay country were not as greatly affected as much of the rest of the Highlands, for Lord Reay was a staunch protestant and had backed the government. Nevertheless great changes did come. The reiving of cattle changed to the droving of cattle south to the trysts as the Highlands became more peaceful and more accessible. With a growing family, who must have watched and discussed the changes that were taking place, and, with his own involvement in farming and his position as ground officer for Durness, James' life must have been active and involved. He died on 30 March 1774, aged sixty-nine years, and is buried in the churchyard at Balnakiel. His widow, Margaret, lived on for another thirty-one years and her name appears on Lord Reay's rent roll of 1789, still as the tenant of Clashneach. She died on 29 September 1805, aged seventy-nine years, and is buried at Balnakiel alongside her husband.

5

Charles Clarke (1767–1831)

Flockmaster, tenant of Glendhu, Glencoul, Kylestrome and Mavidy in the parish of Eddrachillis, and of Achmore, Little Assynt, Cromalt, Kirkton and Unapool in the parish of Assynt. Married Alexina (Lexy) Scobie, Ardvar. Bankrupt in 1824. Died 3 June 1831 aged sixty-four years. Buried in Scourie graveyard.

Children

Family of twelve children; seven boys and five girls, in the space of about twenty-one years.

Thomas (c. 1795–?), tenant of Stronrubie, Inchnadamph in Assynt. Married his cousin, Georgina Clarke, daughter of John Clarke, Eriboll.

Georgina, married Mr Mackinlay.

Hugh (?–1807), tenant of Culkein. Married Margaret Scobie.

James* (1791–1853), emigrated to Tasmania 1825 and farmed Glen Dhu there. Married Jane Mackenzie (1802–1847) of Ledbeg, Assynt in 1829 at Hobart.

Margaret

Jane

John

Hugh (c. 1800–1843), emigrated and farmed Ledbeg, Tasmania. Married Eliza Dixon, (daughter of Captain Dixon, New Norfolk, Tasmania) at Hobart 1836.

Barbara, married Mr Watson.

* Each asterisked name is the subject of a chapter in this book.

Kenneth

Reay, probably emigrated to Tasmania.

Robina (1816–1840), emigrated with her brother Hugh to Tasmania and died there.

In the early autumn days of 1767, the seventh child, a son, was born to James and Margaret Clarke. James was then sixty-four and his wife, Margaret forty-one years old. On 8 September of that year the baby was christened Charles, by Rev John Thomson, minister for fifty years of the large parish of Durness – he gives the greatest length of that parish as being fifteen miles and the greatest breadth as thirteen miles. The Rev John Thomson had been inducted to the parish of Durness three years earlier. Straightaway he had started a register of all the christenings in his parish – and much else besides – carefully signing himself 'John Thomson, Minr' at the bottom of each page.[15]

James Clarke, Charles' father, was becoming a man of substance, although at that time he just held the tack of the small farm of Cnockbreack in the parish of Durness. Margaret, James' wife, was a grand-daughter of Charles Mackay, the third son of the First Lord Reay, who was Chief of Clan Mackay and whose lands embraced the whole province of Strathnaver and of which the parish of Durness formed a part. Strathnaver was vast. Bounded on the west and north by the sea, it stretched from the borders of Caithness in the east to Kylestrome in the west and then south along the watershed. James therefore had close connections with the Chief's family and he was appointed ground officer (local factor) for the parish of Durness. He was also an elder of the kirk. In 1767 – the year that Charles was born – his farming expanded. He moved from Cnockbreack and took the tack of the nearby but larger and better farm of Clashneach on the west side of Loch Borralie.

15 Hew Morrison, *Durness Parish Note*, c.1890.

It was in this pastoral society that Charles grew up and learned the ways of crops and cattle husbandry. Great changes were coming to Highland farming. Tales of new methods came to Durness from the south, from the drovers and from those of the parish who had been away to the wars. They returned telling of the great world outside the province of Strathnaver. There were growing misgivings about the traditional ways of working the land, for hunger was becoming common as the population increased. During the forty-five years from 1772 to 1817, ten years of severe hunger are recorded – almost one year in every five. These were caused by poor harvests followed by very severe winters and late springs. Under the old ways of farming the arable land was not producing enough to feed its increasing human population. Probably the increasing cultivation of potatoes produced the surge in the population which is common wherever that crop becomes a considerable part of that population's diet.[16] All this Charles must have witnessed and he would have looked south across the Kyle of Durness to the 'sheep rooms of the Parph', that great stretch of country where Lord Reay had recently introduced 'Southern' sheep. These were referred to as the 'Great Sheep' to distinguish them from the 'small' or native sheep.

The native sheep were indeed small. They were very few in number compared to the cattle. They were kept largely for their wool which was usually plucked rather than sheared. They were wintered inside the house and kept almost as pets. In 1799 it was written:

> It was an idea long entertained by the inhabitants of the North, that their hills and climate were solely calculated for rearing black cattle; and they had such an inherent prejudice against sheep, and every branch of manufacture, that the few sheep kept by them were left solely to the charge of the women.

16 John Reader, *The Untold History of the Potato*, London 2009.

The 'inhabitants of the North' were correct, as the history of that land over the next three hundred years was to show.

To Charles Clarke, a young man of energy and enterprise, this new system of keeping 'Great Sheep' and herding them outside all the year round must have been of great interest. Lord Reay's sheep on the Parph would probably have been Blackface but Cheviots had also been brought north. Certainly by 1814 Patrick Sellar was stocking his lowland farms on the east coast of Sutherland and his sheep runs in Strathnaver with Cheviots. The body weight and the quantity and quality of wool of these sheep, both Blackface and Cheviot, would have been something quite new to Charles. He would have seized every opportunity to cross the Kyle and see these sheep and the ways that the shepherds had of herding them. Almost all of these shepherds would have come from the south of Scotland, from the Borders. They would have brought with them the husbandry of herding hill sheep and the concept of hirsels, hefts, hefting and regular ages.

On 12 July 1798, at the age of thirty-three, Charles is noted in the baptismal register as the father of a baby, christened Donald, who had been born to 'Mary Mackay, alias nin Dholicalister, Clashneach. n.b.l.w [not born in lawful wedlock]'.[17] He had saved some money by this time and three years later, in 1801, offered a rent of £140 for the sheep farm of Glendhu and Glencoul. This offer was accepted by Lord Reay's factor. Glendhu had first been let as a sheep farm to a Mackay of Bighouse in the late 1780s, who then sub-let it to Colin MacDiarmid, an Argyllshire man. Colin was connected to the chief's family by marriage and was the initiator of this venture into sheep farming. Colin had other interests – trading in cattle and herring fishing – and his management of Glendhu seems to have been faulty. In 1793 he went bankrupt, '. . . partly from inadvertency and, times being bad, unfortunate . . .' The lease was taken over by another man

17 Hew Morrison, *Durness Parish Note*, c.1890.

from Argyll, Alexander Campbell, but he died in 1799.[18] Both
these farmers would appear to have stocked Glendhu lightly for
MacDiarmid had only six hundred ewes and Campbell eight
hundred at their waygoings. Both had failed to make a success
of this farm, perhaps because the knowledge of how to run these
extensive sheep farms was still developing. This would come as
more shepherds came up from the Borders with their inbred
knowledge of herding large flocks on exposed hills.

Sheep thrive on clean ground and ground that has never been
stocked with sheep is where they really thrive. Because Glendhu
had only carried a light stocking of sheep in the twenty years since
first cleared of its small tenants with their cattle, it follows that,
when Charles Clarke first leased that land, it was comparatively
clean and carried a wealth of fine grasses and dwarf shrubs. This
was the legacy left by the years and years of careful seasonal grazing
by the cattle of the tacksman and his small tenants. Sheep have
an extraordinary ability to profit from such clean grazing and
to reward the flockmaster with unusually heavy yields of wool,
good lambing percentages and low levels of loss from disease. The
continuous defoliation by the selective muzzles of thousands of
sheep would in time destroy that fine sward. The sward would
change to one of heather, deer's hair, bents and inferior grasses.
The nature of the place would change as well with the onset of
diseases in the sheep and the rise of ticks and other parasites, but
not yet. Meantime Charles Clarke would take profit from his
growing and thriving flock, grazing his newly leased farm.

Thus Charles, his wife and young family plus a shepherd or
maybe two left Clashneach for Glendhu. He would already have
had some sheep of his own at Durness and these he drove south
for some thirty miles – up Strath Dionard, along to Rhiconich,
on and turning up the Laxford River to Achfary, then south over
the watershed to Glendhu – to the mountains, hills and glens

---

18 Dr Malcolm Bangor-Jones, 'Sheep Farming in Sutherland in the Eighteenth Century', *The Agricultural History Review*, Volume 50, Part II, 2002.

that can be seen today from the Kylesku Bridge. With the sheep covering about four miles or less each day, the journey would have taken at least a week, with Charles, his wife, children and shepherds herding the sheep and sleeping in the heather at night. He was probably able to add to his stock by buying some of the sheep already hefted on Glendhu by the previous tenants.

On arrival on the shores of Loch Glendhu, he may well have had to build or at least repair a house for himself and his wife and family and one or more houses for his shepherds. So, as well as herding the sheep, there would have been the gathering of stones for the building of the houses. It was said that, when you decided to build a house, you worked out the quantity of stones required, doubled it, dug up and carted in all those stones and then you would find that you had just half the stones that were needed. Gathering the stones was hard work but quite straightforward, for there were plenty. Alongside the loch, the ruins of the houses that been the homes of the small tenants would have been an easier source for stones than levering them out of the ground with a tramp pick. The timbers for the roof of the house would have been much more difficult to obtain in that treeless countryside and would require to be imported.

Constant hard work was an accepted part of life, and build that house he did, as well as herding his sheep and cutting his peats. His sheep did well and throve as do any sheep on land that has been previously only lightly stocked. His flock increased greatly in number and Charles would have recruited more shepherds to take over some of the herding from him. He would have introduced the hirsel system to Glendhu and Glencoul, whereby a shepherd was given a part of the farm, a hirsel, to look after and a selected number of wethers or ewes to herd on that hirsel. A hirsel might extend to 3,000 acres or more or less, according to the carrying capacity of the land. Those ewes and their descendents would make that stretch of countryside, that hirsel, their home. The best of the ewe lambs from those ewes would be selected and kept on to replace the older ewes which were getting too old to thrive on the hill. It takes constant herding to get sheep to settle on a hirsel but, once this has been achieved, they will not leave it. Their descendants will follow their dams and become hefted on to that land just like their mothers. There was thus no need for fences or dykes to keep the sheep separate from those of neighbouring hirsels and the shepherd saw to it that his sheep did not stray. He was out on the hill at all hours of daylight and in all weathers herding and the flockmaster made sure his shepherds did just that.

With careful herding and sound management, the sheep throve and Charles prospered. Not only did the sheep do extraordinarily well on his new farm but, at this time of the Napoleonic Wars, the prices for wool and mutton rose to an all-time high. In 1808 he was granted the tenancy of Mauldie and Kylestrome to add to his holding of Glendhu and Glencoul but the annual rent went up from £140 to £380 and then to £480. By 1815 the end of his fifteen year tenancy was fast approaching and he had to agree to an annual rent of £1400 for the next five years until 1820, and thereafter £1600 until 1830, which would be the end of that fifteen year lease. In fifteen years Charles Clarke's rent had multiplied by a factor of ten. In those same years the total annual rents for the whole of Lord Reay's estates had risen from £1321 to £4426.[19] Sheep farming was bringing in far more money to the laird than had ever come from the traditional system of tacksmen, subtenants, cattle and shielings.

There were problems. These new flocks were subject to raids by the dispossessed locals, understandably most discontented at the sight of their homelands being grazed by these sheep. Eleven of the larger sheep farmers formed 'The United Association of the Noblemen and Gentlemen of Sutherland and Caithness for the Protection of Property'. In 1815 a loss of 1,691 sheep was reported, but over the next three years the loss was 'beat down'

19 Dr Malcolm Bangor-Jones, 'Sheep Farming on the Reay Estate', *The Northern Times*, 4 March 1988.

to 853. These figures would be accurate, for shepherds in those days were held accountable for every single sheep in their charge. The loss in these raids must have caused many heated arguments between farmer and shepherd. The 'count' had to be correct and at least once a year there was a 'reckoning'. 'Black Loss' – i.e. sheep which had disappeared without trace – was not accepted and the number of sheep at the end of the year had to tally with those that were there at the start of the year plus births and less sales and recorded deaths. The skin of every sheep that had died had to be produced and handed over to the flockmaster. Any shortfall in the count was worked out and the value of those unaccounted for was deducted from the shepherd's wages.

In the summer of 1818 the painter, William Daniell, was to arrive at Glendhu. Daniell had set out from Land's End in 1813 to journey right round the British Isles, recording views of the coastline by sketches. In summer he travelled and sketched. In winter he returned to London to produce his engravings. He also kept a remarkably detailed diary of his travels. In the parish of Assynt, Daniell was accompanied by George Gunn, the local factor for the Marquis of Stafford. They travelled together, partly by boat along Loch Assynt, from Lochinver to Kirkton where they stayed the night as guests of the minister, Rev Mackenzie. The next day they crossed the watershed to Unapool. Here Daniell left the lands of the Staffords and so parted company with Mr Gunn. Daniell then hired a boat, sailed up Loch Glendhu and landed at the home of Charles Clarke on the northern shores of that loch in the lands of Lord Reay. There was no road to Glendhu but Daniell records how convenient it was to be borne by 'water carriage' to the house of his host.

He stayed a few days with Charles Clarke and records that his host was a man happy and absorbed in his farming while his sons and daughters enjoyed a wide social circle and books, music and conversation. He did not make any sketches at Glendhu, unlike his usual practice of making a sketch of almost every place where he stayed, but noted that it was well named; Glen Dhu, the Dark Glen. It was so narrow and the hills so steep that the house (he calls it a mansion) was shut off from the sun for three months each winter and even in summer there was only a short period of sunshine. Daniell records that Charles Clarke carried a stock of 12,000 to 14,000 sheep on his farms, which must include those tenanted in the Parish of Assynt. Daniel also reports that they did very well although, in times of heavy snowfall, they had to be brought down to the lands beside the sea lochs and to the beaches to feed on the seaweed.

Next day, accompanied by Charles Clarke's son, Captain Clarke, as a guide, they left Glendhu and in pouring rain covered the twenty or more miles to Eriboll in nine hours. They would have gone north over the watershed to Achfary, then climbed to 1500 feet along the ten-mile path to Gobernuisgach, walked through Strath More to cross the Hope River at Cashel Dhu and then finally came down across the Eriboll ground to the farmhouse itself. They had done well. They stayed there with Charles' younger brother, John Clarke, the tenant of Eriboll. After a day's rest the pair went by boat down Loch Eriboll to Rispond where they stayed with James Anderson, Lord Reay's factor.[20]

The idyllic picture of life at Glendhu as described by William Daniell was not to last. Charles Clarke, partly buoyed up by his past successes – and they had been very considerable – and partly because he was forced into it, embarked on a course of further expansion. In 1818 he took over the tenancy of the large sheep farm of Achmore on the northern shores of Loch Assynt from James Scobie, who had gone bankrupt after being tenant there for only six years. Charles then took on the tenancies of the farms of Little Assynt and also of Cromalt, which lies on the south side of Loch Urigill. These farms had previously been tenanted by John Mackenzie, who had also gone bankrupt. Charles had

20 William Daniell, *A Voyage Round the Coasts of Scotland and the Adjacent Isles 1815–1822*.

acted as security for both Scobie and Mackenzie. This meant that he was legally liable for the rents of all these farms and so he had no real choice but to take on the tenancies himself. Charles was now a flockmaster of note and he probably hoped that he would continue to succeed by good farming and careful management. He had been appointed a Justice of the Peace for the county of Sutherland. Because of this and because of his standing in the farming community plus the fact that he now owned stock worth £10,000, the factor for Sutherland Estates agreed to him taking on these additional tenancies. However Charles was not finished expanding his farming, for in that same year he took the sub-tenancy of the eastern half of Unapool and the next year (1819), Cullin and Camore, which together make up Kirktown of Assynt. Twenty-nine subtenants were evicted to enable Charles to farm there and the following year a further twenty-nine were cleared from another part of Unapool to complete his occupancy of the whole of that farm.[21] The scale of Charles Clarke's farming at this time was immense. The list of lands tenanted runs: in the parish of Eddrachillis – Glendhu, Glencoul, Mauldie and Kylestrome; and in the parish of Assynt – Achmore, Little Assynt, Cromalt, Unapool and Kirkton – nine farms in all. Some of his sons would certainly have been old enough by this time to shoulder part of the work of running these farms. Even so, it was a very big handling. It would have covered more than 60,000 acres and was carrying a stock numbering some 14,000 sheep. These were herded by perhaps thirty shepherds, many with boys to help them. In addition to all this he was involved in the fish trade and, no doubt, the droving trade as well.

And then? The high prices and good times did not last. In 1824, at the age of fifty-seven, Charles went bankrupt, as did a good number of other flockmasters at this time. The end of the Napoleonic Wars had brought the returns for wool and mutton

21 Dr Malcolm Bangor-Jones, 'Sheep Farming on the Reay Estate', *The Northern Times*, 4 March 1988.

tumbling down so that the high rents, to which the flockmasters had agreed earlier, could not be paid. The drop in the price of wool was the most serious for it meant the end of the three and four year old wethers – big, hardy sheep that would thrive on the highest and poorest parts of the ground. They were strong enough to break out of deep snowdrifts and lead the ewes out with them. They produced a good clip each year and yielded large joints of mature mutton when the end of their life came but eventually the wether stocks would have to go. Looking far ahead the demand in the future was going to be for fine merino wool, shipped in from Australia and elsewhere, and for young, tender lamb with small joints, shipped in frozen from New Zealand.

Bankrupt, Charles Clarke had to leave Glendhu. He went to live at Oldnay where his older brother, Hugh, had held the tack of Culkein. Hugh had died in 1807 so perhaps Charles ended his days helping his widowed sister-in-law with the working of her land. He had only seven more years to live. He died on a June day in 1831 and lies buried in the graveyard at Scourie, a quiet spot beside a sandy beach near the village.

What of the land? In 1829 all of Lord Reay's land in North West Sutherland was sold by him to the Marquis of Stafford, who became the first Duke of Sutherland in 1833. Glendhu and Glencoul were, of course, included in this sale. In 1870 the sheep were cleared from Glendhu and Glen Coul and the land was turned into a deer forest. The thatched house, which Charles Clarke had built, had tumbled down and a fine new house with a slated roof was built in Glendhu and another in Glen Coul by the sporting tenant – and later the owner – the Duke of Westminster. These housed the stalkers, whose beats were to be a part of the vast deer forests of the Westminster Estate. After World War II these houses fell vacant as stalkers and their families looked for homes with ready access and modern amenities.

The land went back. Looking at those barren hills and glens today stocked with many red deer and maybe a few Blackfaced ewes, it is hard to believe that they could ever have supported sheep farms carrying a large stock of thriving Cheviot ewes and wethers. There are few signs now of the years of the sheep apart from a circular dyke beside the burn below the Allt-an Eas waterfall, which must have been a pen for holding the sheep before plunging them into the pool below to wash the wool before clipping. Today all the grazing is poor. The fertility of that land has gone. There was once a fine sward of grasses, herbs and dwarf shrubs which had been created by the old transhumant cattle economy of the tacksmen and their subtenants. That sward was slowly destroyed by the constant and continuous year-round defoliation of Charles Clarke's great flocks of sheep. No sward can withstand such maltreatment and the speed of deterioration increased when the careful herding of the early years was no longer practised.

It was not the sheep which caused the destruction but the system under which the sheep were kept. The combination of sheep with good grazing husbandry can create fine swards and fertile soils. The pastures of the Romney Marsh in England and of the Canterbury Plains in New Zealand were both created by sheep. Both are fertile and very rich in fine grasses and clovers. The reverse – continuous year-round defoliation of a sward by sheep – will destroy the sward and the fertility of the soil. This is to be witnessed throughout the hills of Sutherland today. This extractive type of sheep husbandry has destroyed the fertility of that countryside. Charles Clarke was not aware of the sweeping ecological changes which his sheep were going to bring to Sutherland. On that day in 1801, when he drove them in to the grazings of Glendhu, like any flockmaster he just came to a halt, called in his dogs, leant on his stick and with great satisfaction watched his sheep eagerly spreading out as they cropped the sweet, clean pastures of that narrow Highland glen.

6
James Clarke (1791–1853)

Born at Clashneach, Durness in 1791. Emigrated to Van Diemen's Land (Tasmania) in 1825 and farmed Glen Dhu there. Special Constable in the Jones River District [Big River or River Ouse?]. Died at Hobart, Tasmania on 10 February 1853. Married Jane Mackenzie (1802–1847) who was born at Ledbeg, Assynt and died at Hobart, Tasmania, 8 March 1847.

Children

Family of twelve children, of whom at least five were to die in infancy or as young children. All were born in the space of seventeen years. Records of children are incomplete but include:

Georgina Margaret (1830–1841), died aged eleven.

Elizabeth Anne Sutherland (1839–1870) who came back to Scotland and married her 2nd cousin, George Granville Clarke, Eriboll.

James was the eighth child in the family of five sons and six daughters of Charles Clarke of Glendhu (1767–1830) and Alexina Scobie of Ardvar. As a child, James would have moved from Clashneach near Durness to Glendhu with the rest of the family in 1801 when his father took on the tenancy of that farm. James would then have been ten years old and it was at Glendhu that he spent his childhood days. His father's farming expanded and, as he grew up, James would have taken on the management of some of his father's other farms across the loch in Assynt. Certainly he met and fell in love with Jane Mackenzie (1802–1847) of Ledbeg

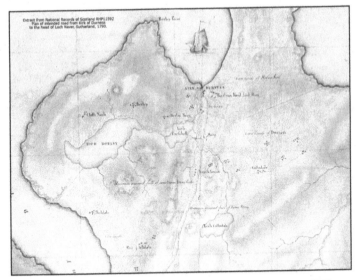

The Cornlands of Balnakiel and Durness, showing run rigs, c. 1790.

at the east end of that parish. One of Charles' farms in Assynt was Kirkton, which is five miles along the road from Ledbeg. If indeed James was involved with the running of Kirkton, then, of an evening, he would often have walked over to see Jane for it wasn't that far.

The bankruptcy of his father, Charles Clarke, in 1824 disrupted the lives of his eleven children, then ranging in age from twenty-five to approximately forty. James decided to emigrate to Australia, to Van Diemen's Land (Tasmania).[22] When he got settled there and had secured a place for them to live, Jane would follow and they would get married but it was going to be four years before that would come about. Did he send a proposal of marriage by letter or did Jane just wait faithfully until James

22 The items that tell the story of James's life in Tasmania – apart from his bankruptcy – were kindly supplied by my niece, Mrs Fiona Mitchell, who obtained them from the library in Hobart. They mainly come from press cuttings from the *Hobart Town Courier* and the *Van Diemen's Land Gazette*.

sent word for her to come out to the colony? However that may be, James took passage on the *City of Edinburgh* and arrived at Hobarton (now Hobart) on 13 April 1825. He was then thirty-four. He soon found employment as a stockman on the stock establishment of Messrs Bethune on the River Ouse, about forty miles north of Hobart. In addition he was appointed a District Constable at Jones River, which lies north of Hamilton. The name of Bethune is interesting. The full name of one of the partners is given as Walter Angus Bethune, listed as having been born in Sutherland in 1794. It is almost certain that James Clarke and Walter Bethune knew each other in their early days back in Sutherland, for Walter was the son of Rev John Bethune D.D., the minister of Dornoch.[23] Walter went to Van Diemen's Land in 1820 and returned the next year to settle. He established there a successful merchant's business, owned several country holdings and seems to have been an established grazier by the time James arrived. Indeed Walter may have written back to James offering him the post of manager of his farms and it was on the strength of this offer that James decided to emigrate. Walter Angus Bethune was a man of importance in Tasmania. He went on to become a member of the Tasmanian Legislative Council and a director of the Bank of Van Diemen's Land.

On 2 March 1827, two years after his arrival in Tasmania, James Clarke applied to the government's Land Board for a grant of land. His assets were £600 in the Bank of Van Diemen's Land plus three hundred sheep, worth 15/- each, making in all £825. In a letter attached to his application James stated that should he receive a grant of land, he would undertake to reside on it immediately and added, 'I beg further to state that my profession in Scotland was Sheep Farming and Agriculture'. At the hearing the governor, Lieutenant General Arthur, wished to know how Clarke had been employed in the colony since his arrival there and was informed that, 'It appears that he has had the entire management

23 *Australian Dictionary of Biography*, Volume 1, 1966.

of the Stock Establishment of Messrs Bethune and is also a District Constable at Jones River'. This satisfied the Lieutenant Governor and on 31 March James was granted eight hundred acres of land with immediate entry. It was autumn and just in time to get the tups out with his ewes. He called his farm 'Glen Dhu'.

His own stock of '300 sheep – worth 15/- each' would have been his 'pack' as a shepherd with Messrs Bethune. It was the custom in Sutherland and in the north of Scotland for shepherds to be allowed to keep a pack as part of their wages. The pack was an agreed number of sheep plus a couple of cows which were the property of the shepherd, not of the flockmaster. They would 'follow the master's flock' or, in other words, they would be herded with the rest of the master's flock and would not receive any special feed or privilege – or at least they were not supposed to. The money from the sale of the lambs and wool produced by the pack went, of course, to the shepherd. Patrick Sellar, the noted east Sutherland flockmaster, wrote how he gave each of his shepherds: 'a cottage and garden, 13 bolls of meal, grass for three cows and a pony, with the profit to be derived from seventy Cheviot sheep of the different sorts, each mixed among the master's sheep of the same kind'.[24] With eleven married shepherds and eight young men employed by him, Sellar reckoned that there were twelve hundred and fifty shepherds' sheep mingled among his own flocks. James would have worked with shepherds' packs back home in Sutherland and would have made sure that he got a pack – and a good one – when he was employed by the Bethunes in Tasmania, hence his flock of three hundred sheep.

James called the property that he had been awarded 'Glen Dhu' after the old home in distant Sutherland and it still goes by that name today. It lies in the basin of the River Ouse and the nearest town is Bothwell. It is good country, although steep in parts with the land rising up to 2000 feet. This part of Tasmania

24 Patrick Sellar, *Farm Reports III County of Sutherland*, Library of Useful Knowledge, 1831.

had long been the home of the Big River Aborigine Tribe. They were probably the last tribe to succumb to British domination but they had now been cleared and the land was ready to be stocked with sheep. Since the early days of settlement in Tasmania, twenty years before, the Aborigines had been a problem for the sheep farmers. The Aborigines were accustomed to a sharing of all resources in a traditional exchange economy. If they came across a sheep while on a hunting expedition, then of course it was speared as a fine dinner for the family. The settlers did not take kindly to natives helping themselves to their sheep and the Aborigines did not take kindly to the white man taking possession of their land. Confrontation became inevitable and the conflict between settler and native became ever more violent. By 1828 the settlers were in a state of fear and Governor Arthur declared martial law. He expelled all Aborigines from the settled districts and virtually gave licence for the Aborigine people to be shot on sight. Then in 1830, a force of 3000 armed settlers, called 'The Black Line', was formed to sweep across the settled part of the island driving the Aborigines before them. Those who were captured were to be re-settled on offshore islands. It was not a great success, for the natives knew the countryside far better than the white man. Many eluded capture. As a District Constable, James would have been involved in this operation. The settlers then turned to the tactic of 'divide and rule'. Tribal raiding and even tribal wars had been a tradition and the settlers now enlisted trackers from one tribe to hunt down the fugitives from the others. In the early 1830s the remnant, said to be just 135 survivors out of the original 5000 native inhabitants, were transported to an offshore island. Although all this may have partly solved the problems connected with the Aborigines, there remained the bush rangers, some of whom were descended from those few convicts who had managed to escape from the penal settlements. These bush rangers formed mounted gangs who made a precarious living by raiding the farms and settlements. As witness to those troubled times, rifle ruts, which are slits built into the walls of the farmhouse from which rifle fire could be directed against attackers, are still to be seen at Glen Dhu.

However, as in Sutherland, the land had been cleared of its native human stock so that sheep could safely graze. And just as in Sutherland where Charles Clarke had entered and stocked Glendhu, which had recently been cleared of those who had lived there for generations, so in Tasmania his son, James, now entered and stocked Glen Dhu, which had recently been cleared of those who had lived there for generations. Just as his father had found fine, clean grazing for his Cheviots, which did well on land that had not previously carried many sheep, so now his son would have fine clean grazing for his Merinos and these were going to thrive on land that had not previously carried sheep.

Meantime Jane Mackenzie arrived at Hobart, having taken passage from Britain in the *City of Edinburgh*, the same ship that had carried James to these new lands five years earlier. She arrived at Hobart on 30 January 1829, accompanied by James' younger brother, Hugh, and James' younger sister, Robina. The three of them had had a long journey from distant Assynt to the port of embarkation and then the voyage south, round the Cape of Good Hope, across the southern Indian Ocean to Australia and finally to dock at Hobart. Jane and James did not waste any time. They were married in Hobart on 4 February, just five days after she had disembarked. She hadn't seen her fiancée for the past five years, in fact not since he had left Assynt in the autumn of 1824. She was twenty-seven and James was thirty-eight. They started their married life in a house on the Bethune property, near enough to Glen Dhu to enable him to herd his sheep on that farm's land as well as managing the lands and flocks of the Bethune partnership.

On 8 April 1829, Hugh appeared before the Land Board and satisfied them that he 'was in possession of £800 Capital', had a brother (James) residing on his Grant at the Big River and that he intended to become a permanent resident settler. He was awarded a grant of 1000 acres, 'subject to the usual conditions'. It was land which marched with Glen Dhu and which he called 'Ledbeg', following the practice of giving the new property a Sutherland name – a name from the old home. Hugh was also leasing a further eight hundred adjoining acres from the Crown. Between them the two brothers were now farming 2,600 acres and James was managing the Bethune's extensive properties as well. The brothers Clarke were building a farming empire, just as their father had done all those years before far away in north west Sutherland.

Next year – in early August 1830 – James was back at the Land Board with an application for a further grant of land. He was reported to be married with one child, but, instead of staying at Glen Dhu, he was residing on and had full charge of all the Bethune's property for which he 'received a salary of £175 per annum plus 5% commission on all sales effected'. He was under an agreement to remain living on Bethune's Grant of Land until Mr Bethune returned from England. This clearly did not please that Land Board. The Board sought to establish farmers who would build houses on their Grant of Land, reside in them and work their land in this cleared countryside. The Board recommended that, as James Clarke was not prepared to reside on his Grant immediately and had not made any great outlay there, i.e., he had not built himself a house on the Grant, he should only receive an extension of two hundred acres to add to the eight hundred that he had been granted three years previously. This was approved by the Lieutenant-General on 5 August 1830. The two brothers were now established graziers and respected men of substance.

In December 1836, Hugh married Eliza, the second daughter of Captain Dixon of Kenmere, New Norfolk, Tasmania. The marriage was only to last for seven years as Hugh died on 16th September 1843 at the home in Hobart of his mother-in-law, Mrs Dixon, 'after a long and severe illness'. However his widow married into another pioneer farming family whose descendants still farm in Tasmania today.

Meanwhile Jane settled down to married life. The life of a pio-neer's wife was a hard one. It may be that Jane did not spend all her years at Glen Dhu, for about 1833 James bought a house in Hobart, which he called Royston. The name Royston may record the connection with Jane's family, the Mackenzies of Ardloch. There is a fine house on the outskirts of Edinburgh and it also is called Royston. There is an inscription above one of the doors of this house which reads: 'Riches unemployed are of no use, but made to circulate are productive of much good'. That may be true but it does rather depend on whether the riches are possessed or borrowed.

Wool prices were good in James' early years at Glen Dhu and his sheep were thriving. This must have given him confidence to expand and extend his interests and his investments. He appears to have borrowed considerably and invested in land both for farm-ing and for development. Let us go back to the early 1800s and the start of the wool trade between Australia and England. It was a Captain McArthur who had first seen the possibilities for the export of Merino wool from Australia. In 1803, then a captain in the army, he had been sent home from New South Wales to stand trial for having wounded a Colonel Paterson in a duel. Fortunately he took with him samples of Australian Merino wool and, on arrival in England, found that the government there was much more interested in Captain McArthur's wool than they were in Colonel Paterson's wounds. The import of fine Merino wool into England from Spain had been brought to a complete halt by the Napoleonic Wars and the north of England wool manufacturers were up in arms over their loss of trade. McArthur drafted a report to the Government which stated that 'the climate of New South Wales is peculiarly adapted to the increase of fine-wooled sheep, and that from the unlimited extent of luxuriant pastures with which that country abounds, millions of these valuable animals may be raised in a few years, with but little other expense than the hire of a few shepherds'. The Government was delighted to help McArthur get this trade under way and he set about doing just that. In 1822 the English Society of Arts awarded him a gold medal for being the first to import a large quantity of wool from Australia into England. The Australian Wool trade was born.

James widened his interests and is recorded in some documents as James Clarke, butcher, in Hobart. James' businesses did well until, in the late 1830s, severe economic depression hit Tasmania hard. The banks restricted credit. Many private individuals and graziers went bankrupt and James was one of them.[25] There is a legal document, dated 19 March 1843, headed: 'In the matter of the Insolvency of James Clarke. Affidavit for the proof of debt due to the Bank of Van Diemen's Land for £1,965/ 4/ 8'.

There had been hard times. His sister, Robina, had died in Hobart on 6 June 1840. She was twenty-four years old. Three years later, on 16 September 1843, his brother, Hugh, also died in Hobart. James and Jane had a family of twelve children, born in the eighteen years of their married life, of which five had died in infancy or in early childhood. On 8 March 1847, Jane herself died at their town residence in Macquarrie Street, Hobart, 'leaving a bereaved husband and a large family of young children to deplore her loss. As a Christian she was most exemplary in all relations of life, and died in the blessed hope of a better world'. She was just forty-five years old.

There followed wearying years of struggle, indebtedness and arrangements for the sale of James' assets. These were very considerable and were first advertised in the *Colonial Times* in August 1843. There were 6,467 acres of land. This was made up of 3,400 acres on the River Ouse, 2,370 acres at Malboro', 730 acres at Sorell, half an acre at New Norfolk and Royston Cottage in Hobart. Royston was later sold for £750. And then there was Glen Dhu – a further 1,400 acres plus six hundred acres in the New Country and the stock – five hundred cattle and 1,950 sheep.

25 I am indebted to and have to thank Professor Pam Rhodes, Hobart University, for all the information on James' financial problems and his bankruptcy. If I have failed to get them correct, the fault is entirely mine.

The sheep were made up of 1,016 grit ewes, 592 gimmers and wethers (two-tooths), 198 pure Saxon ewes and lambs, sixty-nine South Down ewes, twenty Leicester ewes, and fifty-five Saxon and Leicester rams. It looks as though the Saxons, South Downs and Leicesters were all stud sheep. The Saxons would have been of Merino blood and exported to Australia from Saxony. The grand total would seem to have amounted to some 8,467 acres of land, five hundred cattle and 1,950 sheep.

Although the properties and Glen Dhu were first advertised for sale in August 1843, the actual sale of Glen Dhu did not take place until March 1851. Maybe the cash from the sale of the first properties without Glen Dhu satisfied the immediate needs of the creditors and James was left to farm there, possibly with supervision by the bank. Maybe also James (and the bank) saw that Tasmania would climb out of the recession and played for time. Farmers are always optimists even when the laws of economics come into play. Certainly whereas the 1843 advertisement in the *Colonial Times* states that the sale was 'by order of the Assignee to the Estate of James Clarke', the 1851 advertisment in the *Hobart Town Courier* and *Van Diemen's Land Gazette* states, 'Glen Dhu, the property of James Clarke'. There are also differences in the numbers of stock for sale.

The 1851 advertisement for Glen Dhu then continues, 'James Clarke, who is about to retire from the colony'. The homestead was said to be a capital family home with out-offices, a large store barn, stables and every requisite convenience with detached stone cottages for overseer and shepherds. The stock advertised for sale was – 7,000 sheep, fifty cattle plus cart and carriage horses. Then on 9 April of that year, the same paper carried the following news item: 'LAND SALES; – The estate of Glen Dhu, 1,400 acres, the property of James Clarke, was sold on Monday last by Mr Lowes to Mr P. Whyte for £2,500'.

It is very difficult at this distance of time and space to understand how all these transactions worked out. Twenty-four years previously, when the Land Board had made the first award to James, Glen Dhu had been just eight hundred acres of bush. Now it was a thriving pastoral property with farmhouse and buildings. It was a remarkable farming achievement.

As I say, it does look as though the proceeds of the earlier sale may have exceeded his £1965/ 4/ 8 indebtedness. Bankrupt he certainly was (or had been) but one hopes that all the debts were cleared so that there was enough for him to live out his life in Hobart in reasonable comfort. It seems so, for at his death on 10 February 1853 he left enough money to form a trust to care for the needs of the younger members of his family.

Maybe by this time he was not well. There is no more word of him being 'about to retire from the colony' which sounds as though at one stage he had planned to go back to Scotland. James was only to have two years to spend in retirement at Hobart. He died in February 1853 at the age of sixty-two. His death is recorded in the local paper:

Clarke: – On Thursday, the 10th instant at Nile Terrace, Hobart Town, James Clarke, Esq., late of Glen Dhu, Ouse. The funeral will take place tomorrow, Saturday, the 12th instant from his late residence, 4, Nile Terrace. Friends are requested to accept this invitation.

He was sixty-two. During the past thirteen years his wife, five of his children, his sister, and his brother had all predeceased him. Of his twenty-eight years in the colony, while the first fifteen had been pioneering and hard work and success, these last thirteen years had been dogged by bereavement and ill health and indebtedness. Nevertheless he had done well and he still had many of his surviving children around him.

Away back on that autumn morning in March 1827, the Tasmanian Land Board must have been greatly cheered by the sight of James Clarke, a Highland immigrant, thirty-six years old, who clearly possessed ability and a great knowledge of sheep and of their breeding and herding. Here was a man who was just what the colony needed. He would push on and get his Merinos settled to become fruitful and multiply. They would soon be growing wool – fine wool for export to England – on that countryside so recently and successfully cleared of the troublesome Big River Aborigine tribe. And the sheep did well on those clean grazings.

Although James never saw the county of Sutherland again, his daughter, Elizabeth Anne Sutherland Clarke (1839–1870), certainly did. He must have left money for her to make the long journey back to Sutherland for, around 1857 when she was in her late teens, that is where she went. He may have been keen for her to finish her education in Scotland. When she arrived in Scotland she travelled north to see the old family home of Glendhu and her Clarke relations in Sutherland. There she met and married her cousin twice removed, George Granville Clarke, flockmaster at Eriboll, my grandfather. She bore him two sons, George and Jack, and a daughter, Huttie. Elizabeth died in 1870; she was just thirty-one years old. Her tombstone in Balnakiel Churchyard records:

> To the beloved memory of Elizabeth Anne Sutherland Clarke, Wife of George Granville Clarke, Eriboll. Born at Glendhu on the Ouse, Tasmania on 2nd May 1839. Died at Meddat, Ross-shire on 12th June 1870.

There is no sheep stock now on Glendhu in Sutherland. Glen Dhu in Tasmania is still carrying Merinos. In both Sutherland and in Tasmania the natives were cleared from the land to make room for the sheep. In Sutherland today, the sheep and the men who tended them, and their families, have all gone. It is the red deer that graze the land.

7

John Clarke (1770–1837)

Born at Clashneach, Durness, 1770. Flockmaster at Keoldale and at Eriboll. Died at Eriboll on 26 February 1837, aged sixty-seven years. Married Johanna Falconer (1774–1858) daughter of Rev Alexander Falconer, minister of Eddrachillis. Died at Eriboll on 14 January 1858, aged eighty-four years.

Children

A family of eleven children, six boys and five girls, all born in nineteen years:

James (1796–1836), doctor in the service of the Honourable East India Company.

Georgina MacIntosh (c. 1798–?), married her cousin, Thomas Clarke (son of Charles). Thomas was the tenant of Stronchrubie in Assynt.

David Ross (1800–1861), successful merchant in Jamaica. Married Elizabeth Anne Hall in 1827 in Jamaica.

Alexander Falconer* J.P. D.L. (1802–1877), born at Keoldale 1 March 1802. Flockmaster at Eriboll. Died at Rosemount, Tain, 23 August 1877 aged seventy-five. Married Marion Manson (1800–1886), born at Thurso on 19 May 1800. Died at Rosemount, Tain, 7 January 1886, aged eighty-four.

John Falconer (1801–?), doctor in Edinburgh.

Eric Mackay (1806–1849) Major in 3rd Buffs and 17th Regt. Died in Sierra Leone.

* Each asterisked name is the subject of a chapter in this book.

Margaret (1808–?)

Mary MacIntosh (1810–?), married Rev George Tulloch, Edderachillis.

Hughina (1811–1839), married Dr Alexander Skinner. Died in Australia.

Alexandrina (1813–1853), died at Eriboll, 18 January 1853, aged forty years.

Donald Robert (1815–1900), married Mary Wylie. Died in Edinburgh.

John, the youngest child of James and Margaret Clarke, was born and brought up at Clashneach, the farm to which the family had moved three years earlier. The walls of the house are still there on the west bank of Loch Borralie, overlooking that loch. In the days of John Clarke's childhood it would have been a desirable farm, possessed of a light soil and easily worked. Today it is just rough grazing and a part of the outrun of the farm of Keoldale. It is still a kindly and sunny place.

In 1774 when John was only four years old, his father died at the age of sixty-nine years. His mother, Margaret, was then aged forty-eight. She tackled the loss of her husband with courage and energy. She would have had at least five children still at home, ranging from Alexander, being fourteen, Hugh, nine, Charles, seven, Mary, six and John, four. She gave them a good upbringing. The school was less than a mile away at the head of Loch Croispol and there they all learnt to read and write well and to cast accounts. In addition to rearing her family, she ran the farm and is listed as, 'Margaret Clarke, widow of James Clarke, tenant of Clashneach' in the rent roll of Lord Reay's estates for the year 1789.[26] The boys would have helped on the farm and learnt the old ways of working the land and herding the cattle.

26 Angus Mackay M.A., *The Book of Mackay*, 1906.

John married Johanna Falconer around 1800. She was the daughter of Rev Alexander Falconer, minister of the parish of Edderachillis. They were to have a family of eleven children, six boys and five girls, who were all born at Keoldale, except perhaps the youngest, Donald Robert. Lord Reay must have cleared many tenants to be able to create sheep farms like Keoldale. Be that as it may, John entered into the tenancy of Keoldale at Whitsunday 1802, probably with a small stock of sheep – Cheviots or maybe Blackface, the Linton breed as they were then known. Blackfaces were bred and reared in the Cheviot Hills surrounding the village of Linton, near Morebattle in the Borders. Their recognised sale centre was Linton and hence their name. The Cheviot sheep also from the Borders, with their white faces, better wool and larger size, probably arrived in the north around this time. Cheviots were to thrive and stock most of the sheep farms of Sutherland. John farmed Keoldale until 1815. Then, for some now unknown reason, there was a dramatic exchange of tenancies. John and his wife moved from Keoldale to Eriboll while Captain Mackay John Scobie, the tenant of Eriboll, and his wife moved from Eriboll to Keoldale.

Let us go back in time for a moment to the history of Eriboll. Eriboll was cleared over several decades, beginning in the early 1800s. In those years the 7th Lord Reay (1773–1847), the spend-thrift, was chief of Clan Mackay. He needed cash, as did his estates. Sheep would provide that better than his tacksmen with their sub-tenants. Vegetation and soil would change as the husbandry shifted from simple cereal growing on the in-bye with the cattle out on the shielings during the summer to the constant and continuous year-round defoliation of all the land by sheep. The area of land that has been considered as the farm of Eriboll for almost two hundred years, was previously farmed as a number of small farms or townships. These included Heilam, Arnaboll, Eriboll itself, Strabeg and, of course, Strathmore. Donald Mackay, who gave evidence to the Highlands and Islands Commission in 1883, was born in

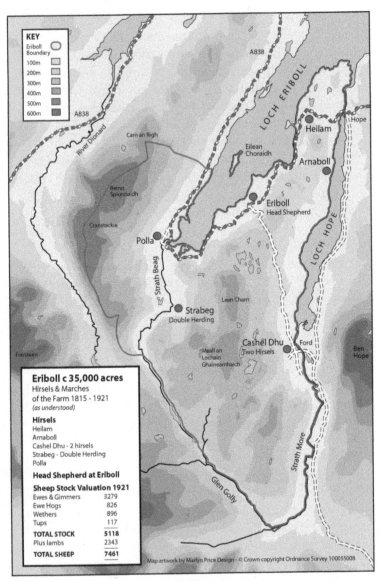

KEY
Eriboll Boundary
100m
200m
300m
400m
500m
600m

A838

LOCH ERIBOLL

River Dionard

Carn an Righ

Beinn Spionnaidh

Cranstackie

Foinaven

Polla

Strath Beag

Strabeg
Double Herding

Lean Charn

Meall an Lochain Ghaineamhaich

Glen Golly

Eilean Choraidh

Heilam

Arnaboll

Eriboll
Head Shepherd

Cashel Dhu
Two Hirsels

Ford

LOCH HOPE

Strath More

Hope

Ben Hope

Eriboll c 35,000 acres
Hirsels & Marches
of the Farm 1815 - 1921
(as understood)

Hirsels
Heilam
Arnaboll
Cashel Dhu - 2 hirsels
Strabeg - Double Herding
Polla

Head Shepherd at Eriboll

Sheep Stock Valuation 1921

Ewes & Gimmers	3279
Ewe Hogs	826
Wethers	896
Tups	117
TOTAL STOCK	**5118**
Plus lambs	2343
TOTAL SHEEP	**7461**

Map artwork by Marlyn Price Design - © Crown copyright Ordnance Survey 100055008

The farm of Eriboll showing the marches and the hirsels, 1815–1921.

Strathmore.[27] His family was cleared from there, 'just before I was born', which would be around 1820 or maybe earlier. They were removed to Strabeg where they lived until they emigrated to Nova Scotia in 1832. When Donald grew up he moved around the world to New Zealand, Rogart, Argyll and then back to Laid. He states in his evidence that, before Strathmore was cleared, all that strath was farmed from Gobernuisgach down to the ferry at Cashel Dhu and, 'there would be 200 souls living there at any rate.' The other farms must also have been home to many souls. In total, what is now Eriboll could have had an established population of perhaps five hundred and they were not starving. Certainly there were bad harvests. The grain from the 1740 harvest had run out by the summer of 1741 and the people tried to survive on milk and fish. Dysentery became rife and 10% of the population died. However the harvest of 1741 was plentiful and the people soon recovered.[28] There is a condition in livestock husbandry, both cattle and sheep, called compensatory growth. If an animal has been on very short rations for a period and has lost weight and condition, when it is brought back onto a full and fair diet that animal will thrive and make up or even surpass the condition it would have been in had a normal diet always obtained. Does this apply to the human race? I don't know. In the Highlands, poor harvests were not that uncommon but the people recovered and life went on. How else did the widow from Strathmore succeed in rearing her six sons so that the smallest of them was over six feet in height? Robb Donn, the Gaelic poet, was born and reared in that strath. There is no hint in his poetry of being in the least constrained by hunger. The careful peasant husbandry of run rig and shielings, practised in that countryside, fed the people for most of the year. For those days they were a healthy, virile community.

At that time Major Donald Mackay was the tacksman at Eriboll and he was also a successful drover as were many of the

27 Napier Commission, 1886.
28 Napier Commission, 1886.

larger tacksmen. He had risen to the rank of major in the Duke of Gordon's North Fencibles and is described by Dr John Kennedy, whose father was the missionary at Eriboll, as, 'A gentleman, a soldier, a Highlander and a Christian at once'. In the 1770s Major Mackay built a new house there and carried out various improvements. His daughter, Barbara (1775–1854) married Captain Mackay John Scobie (1774–1818). Mackay John Scobie had been in the East India Company's Service. He then became tacksman, first of Melness and, possibly when his father-in-law died, of Eriboll. In 1815 they moved from Eriboll to Keoldale (while John Clarke and his wife moved from Keoldale to Eriboll) but Mackay John Scobie died there three years later in 1818 and is buried at Balnakiel. Barbara lived on, almost certainly at Keoldale, for another thirty-six years and, like Margaret Clarke at Clashneach, would have reared her family and managed the farm. Keoldale was bought by the Board of Agriculture in 1919 and turned into a sheep stock club for returned Durness ex-servicemen. That sheep stock club is still there today and is successful.

The reason for this exchange of tenancies between Keoldale and Eriboll is still not known, nor is it known whether the sheep stocks on these farms remained where they had been bred or were moved. It is likely that the flocks stayed where they were. There would then have been interesting valuation negotiations as to the worth of each flock. However, if the stocks were moved, there would have been the serious problem of getting them to settle on their new hirsels. Whatever the reason for the exchange, in 1815 the Scobies did move to Keoldale and the Clarkes did move to Eriboll. There, at Eriboll, John and his wife, Johanna, started the Clarke family's tenancy of that farm which was going to last for the next 106 years. On the day of the flitting, there must have been two processions of parents, children, servants, household goods, horses, dogs and farm stock – the Scobies travelling westwards and the Clarkes travelling to the east. Where did they cross over? Did they get the ferry over the loch or did they cross the hill?

Let's hope they had a good dry day for the journey – twenty miles round the coast and across the loch or ten miles over the hills. It must have been a subject for discussion for many a year to come and indeed was still being talked of locally forty years ago.

In 1815 the farm of Eriboll extended to some 35,000 acres and included what is now part of the grazings of the Laid township. These grazings were removed from Eriboll in early 1830s but the rest of the marches appear to have remained almost unchanged until the Clarke's waygoing in 1921. It is understood that the farm's western march stretched from the mouth of a burn that entered the loch about two miles north along Loch Eriboll from Polla, right round that loch to the headland, Rubh'a'Mhuilt, near the mouth of the Hope River. The beach on this long coastline of some ten miles gave the farm most valuable access to seaweed in times of snowstorm. The limestone island, Eilean Choraidh, was included in the farm of Eriboll although it lay much nearer to the crofting township of Laid than to Eriboll itself. This island had been home to a number of several small tenants at one time. However they had been cleared by Lord Reay and the island was then added to the new Eriboll sheep farm. The east march of the farm ran up the middle of the Hope River, the *medium filum* in legal terms, then along the length of Loch Hope to the ford at Cashel Dhu and hence along the Strathmore River to below Gobernuisgach. Here the march turned north westwards and climbed up Glen Golly, over the watershed and down into Strath Coille na Fearna. The march then climbed to the heights of Cranstackie, along the watershed to Meall nan Cra from where it ran down the burn referred to earlier, back to the shore of Loch Eriboll about two miles along the loch from Polla.

Eriboll was a great sheep farm. The arable land where the small farming tenants had grown their crops, the former shielings where their cattle and other livestock had summered, the outcrops of limestone and the heather hills plus the ten miles of beach with its seaweed added together to create a blend of grazings for all seasons of the year. For the next hundred years the flockmasters and their shepherds would use the resources of this land with diligence and skill to breed one of the finest flocks of North Country Cheviots in the county of Sutherland. Eriboll was divided into the following hirsels – Heilam, Arnaboll, two hirsels at Cashel Dhu, a double herding in Strabeg and the eild herding of Polla.

John's thirteen years' tenancy of Keoldale had gone well. The Napoleonic war in Europe had brought a rising market for wool, as the import of wool into this country from Europe had stopped. There was also a good demand for the wethers and for the store cattle of the Highlands. These were driven south to the pastures of England to be sold when fat, many as beef for salting for the Royal Navy. John and Johanna and their family settled down in the tacksman's house at Eriboll. It was here that Johanna reared their family of six boys and five girls, all born in the space of nineteen years. John got on with running the farm.

Whitsun 1815 was not a good time to start in to the tenancy of a new sheep farm. The previous thirteen years of the tenancy at Keoldale had been prosperous. Based on the high prices going at that time for wool and for store cattle, John had offered a very high rent for Eriboll. Indeed he may well have outbid Captain Scobie. Farmers are always optimists when considering future profits. However with the family safely flitted, the shepherds engaged and, most important of all, the sheep stock settled on their hirsels under the new regime, John would have been pleased with his move. Eriboll was a good farm. The land was still clean. The sheep were thriving. He was on good terms with his landlord, Lord Reay. Yet, as so often happens in farming, this idyllic existence was not going to last. Far away from Eriboll, Napoleon lost the battle of Waterloo in June of that very year and the war, that had for so long stopped all trade with Europe, came to an end. Prices for both wool and cattle fell seriously. Many flockmasters in Sutherland soon found that they could not pay the rents to which they had agreed during the boom wartime years. A number went bankrupt, including John's older brother, Charles, who was tenant of Glendhu, Glencoul and a number of other farms. John survived. He seems to have agreed with Lord Reay a nineteen-year lease at an annual rent of £800 in 1815. By 1823 he was three or more years behind with his rent and appears to have owed Lord Reay the sum of £2193: 6: 8 for these arrears of rent. He had to call on his two elder sons for help. His financial affairs were certainly complicated as the statement from Mr R. M. Murray, Bank Agent with the British Linen Bank in Tain, shows.[29] And it got worse.

In those days there was not much scope for cutting costs on a hill farm in Sutherland. The main expenditure was the rent. The rest of the costs – wages, running costs and personal expenses – were low in comparison. It was only after the Second World War that agricultural economists came up with the idea of ranching hill farms to offset the large increases in shepherds' wages. Then two, three or even more hirsels were all put under the charge of one shepherd and the careful herding of former times was abandoned. This was not an option in 1823 and anyway, in those days, it was not the shepherds who were expensive. No, the only hope was to keep well in with the landlord and especially with his factor.

John's second son, David Ross Clarke (1800–1861), was doing well, working in a merchant house in Jamaica. He backed his father with a guarantee. He wrote to Lord Reay:

Kingston, Jamaica March 6 – 1826

My Lord,

I have not the honour of being personally known to your Lordship, but the circumstance which calls upon me to address you will, I am sure, be deemed by your Lordship a sufficient excuse for the liberty taken.

29 Scottish National Library, *Sutherland Collection.* I am indeed indebted to Dr Malcolm Bangor-Jones for obtaining all these documents and information for me. Without his help, this book would never have been written. If I have got anything wrong, then the fault is entirely mine.

My father writes of his having fallen considerably in arrears of rent to your Lordship, from the pressure of the times of late years; and of having applied to your Lordship for relief. He states to me an arrangement proposed to be made in his favour by your Lordship, wherein your Lordship consents to strike off the Amount of Arrears, and make a reduction in the annual rent of the Farm of Eribol, on condition that he pay to your Lordship £1500. sterling in ten years, by annual instalments of £150. – your Lordship asking as securities for the due payment thereof his two sons, James and myself.

My father has, I believe, on all occasions experienced from your Lordship the greatest kindness, indulgence and condescension; and such of his family as have had the good fortune to be known to your Lordship have been much gratified at the kind notice you were pleased to take of them which, joined to the very liberal and handsome manner in which, on the present occasion, your Lordship comes forward to relieve your tenant, is most deserving of our gratitude. Your Lordship's considerate kindness in proposing as the securities of your tenant, his two sons (of whose circumstances your Lordship could not have much knowledge) shall not soon be forgotten by us – and, I have now much pleasure in saying that I have no hesitation in lending my name towards the perfecting of the arrangement in question – My brother, I have no doubt, will be equally ready to do so.

For your Lordship's satisfaction, it may be proper for me to state that I am connected with one of the most respectable Mercantile Houses here, William Middleton & Co., and Middleton & Tenant in Glasgow – and in the course of time, if I should be blessed with Health, I have reason to hope that my circumstances may be very comfortable.

I pray your Lordship to excuse my trespassing so much on your time.

I have the honour to be, My Lord, with the highest respect

Your Lordship's most obedt. Sevt.   D. R. Clarke

To The Right Honble Lord Reay

It is a splendid letter! His old schoolmaster back in Durness would have been proud of him. His elder brother, James, was a doctor and must also have written and agreed to act as a guarantor for their father. With these two sound guarantees, John was not turned out of Eriboll but continued there as tenant, farming under this burden of debt.

Then in 1829 came the next crisis. Over the years the Marquis of Stafford had advanced large sums to Lord Reay. Lord Reay was failing to keep up the interest payments just as his tenants were failing to keep up the payment of their rents to him. In order to settle this matter, the Marquis agreed to take over the lands which still remained in Lord Reay's ownership, in exchange for writing off Lord Reay's indebtedness. These lands were the parishes of Eddrachillis, Durness and Tongue and included, of course, Eriboll. Rather in contrast to Lord Reay's estates, the Sutherland estates were well and efficiently run. There were factors and James Loch, as commissioner, supervised them. There was close accounting and excellent record-keeping and filing. There was also the determination and the drive to develop the Sutherland Estates.

In 1832 James Loch commissioned Patrick Sellar to make a survey of 'Durness, and certain parts of Tongue, Farr and Reay' – in other words the Duke's purchase of 1829. There was to be no hanging about. Loch's letter of instruction to Sellar is dated 3 January 1832. Sellar's survey was completed and his report was written up and signed at Morvich on 15 May 1832, just four and a half months later. It makes most interesting reading: 'I found in the Reay Country, the pastures better, good part of the tillage land of finer staple, & the fish of higher quality and more abundant, than in this part of Sutherland; yet the stock inferior, the Rents Lower, and the universal people in comparative indigence.' He approves of Lord Reay's earlier clearances: 'One thing Lord Reay has done to your hand. He has thoroughly ejected the people from the sheep walks, and settled them along the Shores of the Estate; and I think, it, chiefly, remains for you, at this Stage to determine, how these Sheep walks can be made to produce the greatest value of Sheep and Wool.'

He goes on to devote a third of his report as to how Eriboll can be improved. His comments on Eriboll are of great interest. He reports that, 'Eriboll Farm will never yield a fleece or a sheep equal in weight or value to what ought to be produced by the mountains surrounding Dureness Loch, and by the Parph. It consists of Six herdings of hard, sound, and well proportioned land; and will carry, in Great Safety, a short, tight, handsome sheep, bearing a very fine fleece of light weighting wool.' He continues, 'Its herdings are well arranged – the Ewes on Eriboll, Feulin, and Badivoir; hogs on Hilum; Gimmers on Polla; and Wethers on Strathmore.' It seems that the system at that time was to run the hoggs on Heilam, next year move them as gimmers to Polla and the following year back to the ewe hirsel where they were born.

What a lot of herding! It seems that the practice of putting the ewe hoggs, when they returned from wintering, straight back on to the hirsels where they had been born had not yet been developed. That would have saved a great deal of herding for they would have readily hefted and settled there for the rest of their lives. Yet these moves between three hirsels did mean that, when growing up, these future ewes got the benefit of various swards and their different minerals. The problems of mineral deficiencies had not been scientifically examined but, clearly, the pining they can cause had been observed by the flockmasters and their shepherds. This movement to different hirsels gave the growing sheep something of the essential trace elements which are needed to bring health and the desirable growth of frame. Hence the acceptance of arduous herding, to produce a fine ewe stock.

Sellar recommends that the four ewe and hogg herdings should be worked by shifts as: 'By this, I expect they will Save one or two hundred hoggs, which seem, yearly, to die of the sickness.' What was the sickness? Possibly pining, which is now controlled by dosing with trace elements or by boluses which are coated with minerals and which slowly release these when placed in a sheep's stomach. Or it may have been braxy. Certainly some limited control of braxy could be obtained by careful control of grazing until injection with prophylactic vaccines was introduced in the mid-1900s. These vaccines then revolutionised the health care of hoggs and all the other ages of sheep. It may have been both, or a combination of the many diseases that can afflict sheep, especially young sheep, and which diligent herding can do so much to control.

Sellar's second recommendation was to move the farmer's residence from Eriboll to Polla where a hundred acres of 'drowned land await the draining spade, the plough, and the limestone from Eriboll Island to grow whatever crops are required on the farm.'[30] This was never carried out. However those one hundred acres were to benefit in the years to come from the draining spade for, in the lower part of Strabeg, a length of the Polla River does run in an unusually straight channel, while a small portion of that river still follows a meandering course. There is good, deep land in lower Strabeg alongside the Polla River and it had – and still has – the potential to grow whatever crops are required on the farm.

30 Staffordshire Record Office. *Report by Patrick Sellar, concerning Durness, and certain parts of Tongue, Farr and Reay surveyed by him, in consequence of a letter received from James Loch Esquire, dated 3d. January 1832.*

His third recommendation was to sow with grass all the land that was then in tillage at Eriboll. He says that oats, potatoes and turnips can be bought from Caithness, Sutherland or Ross, cheaper than can be grown at Eriboll but, 'the medicine of Sweet Grass required on a mountain farm, to "turn" the weak end of the Ewes, Lambs and Small dinmonts and Gimmers, you cannot have, Unless you allow it to Grow.' Well yes, perhaps; but I don't think that I wholly agree with that proposition – particularly laying all the arable land at Eriboll itself down to grass!

A New Lease

> Poor tenant bodies scarce of cash
> How they maun thole the factor's snash.
> He'll stamp and threaten, curse and swear
> He'll apprehend them, poind their gear,
> While they maun stan, wi' aspect humble
> And hear it a' and fear and tremble.

> Robert Burns

The nineteen year lease of Eriboll had been entered into in 1815 and was to end in 1834. There was doubt as to whether the estate was prepared to enter into a new lease with John Clarke. However Alexander, thirty-two years old, was now a partner with his father in the farm and he was bringing drive and enterprise into the running of Eriboll. Further, the above largely favourable report by Patrick Sellar on the management of Eriboll must have given confidence to the commissioner, James Loch, that Eriboll was being well farmed.

The clipping list for 1833 gives the sheep stock of Eriboll as:

Ewes		2020
Gimmers	680	2700
Old wethers		420

Young wethers	520	
Dinmonts	610	1550
Tups	50	
Tup hoggs	19	<u>69</u>
Total clipped in 1833		4324
(error; correct figure is 4319)		
Less sales of 1833:		
Wethers	400	
Ewes	420	<u>−820</u>
		3504
Lambs speaned in 1833		1550
(77%: lambs to ewes at clipping)		
Total sheep on Eriboll at		
Martinmas 1833		5054
Loss on the whole stock		
from clipping 1833 to		
Whitsunday 1834		−482 (9%)
(calculated from an average)		
Total sheep on the Farm at		
Whitsunday 1834		4572

The value of the livestock is then shown as:

4572 sheep @ 15/-	£3429
10 Cows @ £10 each is	£80
(error; correct figure is £100)	
2 Bulls @ £10 do is	£20
20 Young Cattle at £3	£60
10 Horses at £10	£100
Alex Clarke's cattle	£80
Value of the Stock at	
Whitsunday 1834	<u>£3769</u>
(exclusive of farming implements	
and household furniture)	

Alexander writes:

If it should please the Noble Proprietor to give us a New Lease of Eriboll I can show to Mr Loch's satisfaction that at Martinmas first, we would not be in debt £10 in any way whatsoever, except the debt to the Noble Proprietor, and the British Linen Co. With respect to the debt to the Noble Proprietor, were we continued as tenants, I would find security for paying the whole in three Instalments within three years after Whitsun 1834.

With respect to the Cash Acct. to the Brit. Lin. Co., I have an assurance that were we continued as tenants, that ample time would be given us to pay it up.

And may I also state that in Sept. first I propose to dispose of by Roup, all the extra Black Cattle and horses on the Farm, the proceeds probably £200, to be equally shared in lessening the debt to the proprietor and the Bank.

Signed. Alex. Clarke

There is also:

A View of the Affairs of Jno. & A. Clarke, Eriboll as at Whitsunday 1834.

In Acct. With the Duke of Sutherland

To amount paid by His grace to Lord Reay for arrears,
    at purchasing the Estate, supposed: £1500: : :

To int. Thereon to Martinmas 1834, being 5 years
    at 4 p cent   300: : :

To 6 years rent, from Whitsunday 1829 to Whitsunday 1834,
    supposing an abated Rent of £500 p. annum will
    Only be charged   3000: : :

To Cash advanced by Mr Horsburgh at different times
    289:14: 2

By Paid Mr Horsburgh in 1829	772: :
By Paid do. in 1830	490: :
By Paid do. in 1831	850: :
By Paid Mr Baigie in 1832	800: :
By cash to be paid out of sales of 1833	850: :
By Meliorations as pr lease £1000, but if the abated rent is only charged will be satisfied with	500: :
By Balance due the Duke of Sutherland at Whitsun 1834, when lease expires	827:12: 2
	£5089:14: 2
To balance due to the Duke of Sutherland as above	£827:12: 2
To Cash account due to the Brit. Lin. Co with Int to 30th May 1834	903: 6: 6
By Value of Stock as subjoined State	3769: : :
By Surplus at Whitsunday 1834 in favour of the Messrs Clarke	2048: 1: 4
	£3769: : :

(The addition of the final figure is incorrect. It should be £3,779: :)

(Scottish National Library, *Sutherland Collection*)

It is complicated. The partnership's assets exceeded their debts by £2038: 1: 4 (when the addition is done correctly). I wonder who prepared the statement. I think that I can see the hand of the bank agent of the British Linen Bank in Tain but it was young Alexander Clarke who was the driving force behind gathering the facts and presenting the case for the renewal of the lease of Eriboll. It worked.

The Clarkes were granted a new lease of Eriboll and, on 27 July 1834, James Loch wrote to the Duke of Sutherland:

I have much satisfaction in saying that by a letter I have from Young Clark (sic) at Eriboll, he says from the good prices obtained these last two years, his father's debts will be all very nearly p[ai]d up at Martinmas – leaving him a valuable stock capital to go on with – we have thus I hope saved one tenant by indulgence. An old family of the district.[31]

Farming was coming out of the slump which followed the ending of the Napoleonic Wars, prices were improving and the outlook was better. However old John Clarke was not to be spared for very long to enjoy this change of fortune. He was now sixty-four and perhaps rather worn out by struggling with his indebtedness over these last ten years. In 1837, just three years later, he died. His coffin was probably carried by ferry across Loch Eriboll – just as, twenty-two years earlier, he had travelled in the other direction when he moved from Keoldale. It was then taken along the road to Durness and on to the churchyard at Balnakiel, where he was buried beside his father. He had farmed Eriboll well and left it with a valuable sheep stock – James Loch said so. His widow, Johanna, was to live on at Eriboll for another twenty-one years, dying there in 1858 at the age of eighty-four.

31 Scottish National Library, *Sutherland Collection*. Again I am indebted to Dr Malcolm Bangor-Jones for providing me with all this information on the negotiations for a new lease of Eriboll. And again, if I have made errors in describing these, the fault is entirely mine.

8

Alexander Clarke (1802–1877)

Born at Keoldale, 1 March 1802. Flockmaster at Eriboll. A Deputy Lieutenant for the County of Sutherland and Justice of the Peace. Hon. Secretary, North and West of Sutherland Farmers Club and Surveyor of Taxes. Superannuate Officer for Station for R (Revenue?) and Taxes.

1841 census: Farmer: 90 acres arable; about 55,000 acres pasture. Employing twenty-four labourers and shepherds.

1851 census: Sheep Farmer: employing eleven shepherds, three ploughmen, four labourers.

1861 census: Farmer of 50,000 acres hill and pasture and 100 acres arable. Employing twenty shepherds and labourers.

Died at Rosemount, Tain on 23 August 1877, aged seventy-five years. Married Marian Manson (1800–1886), daughter of Dr Alexander Manson, Thurso, born at Thurso on 19 May 1800, married on 8 July 1828. She died at Rosemount, Tain on 7 January 1886, aged eighty-six years.

Children

A family of eight children, five boys and three girls; all born in the space of thirteen years:

Alexander Manson (1829–1878), farmed Meddat. Captain, Highland Militia. Married Emily Walter, daughter of Rev. Edward Walter, Rector of Langton, Lincolnshire.

John M.D. (1831–1861), Assistant Surgeon, H.M. 13th Light Regiment. Died at sea on passage home from India, aged thirty years.

George Granville Leveson-Gower (1833–1904), born at Eriboll. Flockmaster at Eriboll. Farmed Meddat. Major in Militia. Father of James Clarke (NBLW), whose mother was Johann Macdonald. Married (1) Elizabeth Anne, cousin (2) Sophia Jane Walter (3) Alice Gibson. Died in Edinburgh.

Johanna Falconer (1834–1858), died at Eriboll on 3 November 1858, aged twenty-four years.

Janet (1836–?), tutor at Eriboll, married Macmillan (?).

Jemima (1838–1927), not married.

David Ross (1840–1908), Captain; Bengal Staff Corps. Married Mary Tulloch.

Eric Donald (1842–1875), Captain 75th Stirling Regiment. Died at East London, South Africa on 27 February 1875, aged thirty-three years.

Alexander, the fourth child of John and Johanna Clarke, was born at Keoldale and moved to Eriboll with the family in 1815 at the age of thirteen. Both his two elder brothers left home when young. James (1796–1836) became a doctor in India and David (1800–1861) a successful merchant in Jamaica. Their father provided the funds to launch them on their careers. Alexander stayed at home and lived at Eriboll all his life. By his letter-writing he had clearly had a good education and he grew up to be a man of great ability and energy. His was the life of being a leading flockmaster in the County of Sutherland, a Deputy Lord Lieutenant for that county and a Justice of the Peace. As their finances improved the Clarkes spent more time in lowground Easter Ross, especially in the winter, and acquired tenancies of two arable farms down there to complement their farming of Eriboll. He died in 1877, aged seventy-five years, at Rosemount, a substantial house with a farm attached about two miles south of Tain.

As described in the previous chapter, his father had to undertake difficult and protracted negotiations over the future of the tenancy of Eriboll with his landlord, Eric Donald, 7th Lord Reay, and with his factor. Rental and tenancy negotiations are always fraught – today just as they were then. Lord Reay was a spendthrift. He was constantly trying without success to get his estates to produce enough cash to cover his personal expenses and the interest payments on his very considerable debts. By 1824, Alexander's father was also in financial trouble. He was several years in arrears with the rent and faced being turned out of Eriboll. Alexander, then aged twenty-two, would have witnessed the associated comings and goings and almost certainly took an active part in the discussions. Guarantees for reducing the sums outstanding on the rent were pledged by his two elder brothers and the negotiations were eventually successful. The lease of Eriboll was renewed and the Clarkes continued as tenants of Eriboll.

Certainly the times were hard. The Napoleonic War had ended and prices had fallen seriously. Farmers and their landlords were all hard up. When times had been good with wartime prices, many tenants had agreed inflated rents. Now they had to find the money to pay these rents and money was scarce. However the discipline of thrift and careful management in the running of Eriboll prepared young Alexander for those difficult days. Around this time he became a partner with his father in Eriboll and, on 8 July 1828, he married Marion Manson. She was a doctor's daughter from Thurso and they were to have a family of eight children, all born at Eriboll.

Next year, 1829, Lord Reay disposed of his lands at Durness and elsewhere to the Marquis of Stafford, being deeply indebted to him. With this transfer of ownership, great changes would then occur in the Reay Country. The Marquis of Stafford and the organising ability of his Sutherland Estate management would bring a very different approach to the management of these lands and their people.

This acquisition of Lord Reay's estate was followed by a period of energetic development activity. It was led by James Loch, the commissioner for the Marquis of Stafford's estates. The countryside was lacking in roads, bridges, ferries and buildings. Straightaway a road was built from the Kyle of Tongue to the River Hope – three miles of it through the peat bogs and the desolation of the A'Mhoine. Halfway along that road, Moine House was built to serve as a refuge for travellers. At the Hope River, a chain ferry was installed with a sloping ramp on each bank whereby horses and carriage could be driven on board, carried over the river and discharged on the far side, all without any unyoking of the horses. A house for the ferryman, convenient to the crossing, was also built. From this ferry the road was continued around Loch Eriboll, with a very fine two-arch bridge across the Polla River, and on to Durness. A carriage could then be driven, without the passengers ever disembarking, from the Kyle of Tongue to the Kyle of Durness. A passenger ferry across Loch Eriboll was established from Heilam to Portnancon and, again convenient to that ferry, a house for the ferryman was built at Ard Neackie with the Stafford coat of arms engraved above the door. When all these developments were complete, the natives must have found the ease of access to Eriboll and Durness quite extraordinary, having always accepted that struggling through peat hags and wading burns and rivers was normal travel.

Patrick Sellar enjoyed at least some of these facilities as he journeyed on his survey of these lands for the estate in 1832. His report on that survey with its note: 'It [Eriboll] consists of six herdings of hard, sound, and well proportioned land; and will carry, in Great Safety, a short tight, handsome sheep fleece, bearing a very fine fleece of light weighting wool. Its herdings are well arranged . . .'[32] If Sellar saw something of which he did not approve, he was not slow to criticise it. Therefore his approval

32 For a more complete account of Patrick Sellar's report, please see previous chapter (Chapter 7).

in the main of the way that Eriboll was being run must have considerably helped the Clarkes in the next year's negotiations for the renewal of their lease as is described below.

1833 was a momentous year. George Granville Leveson-Gower, Marquis of Stafford and 1st Duke of Sutherland, died on 19 July of that year at the age of seventy-five. Alexander's third son was then born in November and was christened 'George Granville Leveson-Gower' in honour of his father's recently deceased patron. Around this time the 2nd Duke presented Alexander with a very fine elephant tooth snuff box, inlaid with gold, maybe as a christening present for George Granville. There was mutual respect here between tenant and landlord. Alexander was delighted with the new roads and bridges, which supported his farming, while, to the Duke, Alexander represented the very type of progressive and energetic young farmer that he wanted to see as tenants of his Sutherland farms. The Duke was coming under pressure from the public's growing resentment of the clearances. It must have given him satisfaction to see Eriboll being well run and successful. It was not so satisfactory for those who had been cleared. Also in 1833, negotiations for a new lease of Eriboll started with James Loch, the commissioner for the Duke of Sutherland's estates. The existing lease had been for nineteen years from 1815 and so it was due for renewal the next year, 1834.

It is likely that it was Alexander who led the negotiations with James Loch and it was certainly Alexander who prepared the accounts of the partnership's financial position. These are described in Chapter 7. The negotiations must have been difficult, for the Clarkes' finances were in a bad way. However Alexander made out a strong case for continuing the tenancy and the negotiations were in the end successful. Loch was clearly impressed with Alexander and said so in his letter to the Duke of 27 July 1834, of which the text is given in Chapter 7.

The new lease for the next nineteen years was duly signed and Alexander settled down to farm Eriboll. He began to thrive, thanks to his skilled and careful management of Eriboll and to the improving financial climate of the times. As has been related in Chapter 7, his father died in 1837 at the age of sixty-seven, probably worn out with farming under such a heavy load of debt.

Luib Bhan

On the morning of 11 July 1837, Alexander set out for Altnaharra, riding from Eriboll over the Craigan to Strathmore. There he saw to his horror that his neighbour, Mr Paterson, tenant of Melness, had engaged workmen who had started to build a stone embank-ment or dyke across the Strathmore River, half a mile upstream from Mhuiseil. That river was the boundary between Eriboll on the west bank and Melness on the east. The legal definition of such a river boundary was, and still is, the medium filum (the middle of the thread). In other words the march between the farms was the middle of the river. If the river shifted its course or its course was moved, then one farm would gain some land and the other farm lose the same. Alexander writes that, '. . . if it [the new dyke] stands, this will have the effect of throwing the water on the opposite side and destroying some of our best lands'. The lands referred to were the Luib Bhan, some twenty to thirty acres of most kindly haugh land. Every year in the spring the sheep would have been carefully kept off this grassland until the lambing started so that a green bite would come away. The Luib Bhan would then be the very place to put the milk on a newly lambed ewe.

That July morning Alexander rode on to Altnaharra from where he penned a letter, reporting these goings-on to the factor at Tongue, Mr Robert Horsburgh, Ten days later, on the morn-ing of 21 July, he was again writing to Mr Horsburgh, this time from Eriboll, saying that he would write to Mr Paterson, tenant of Melness: '. . . proposing that he desist until you come to the spot; if he refuses to do so, or that if you decline interfering, my only alternative would be to get an interdict and lay this correspondence before His Grace's law agent . . .'. It was the factor's job to sort out this kind of problem and he was clearly not getting round to doing so. Alexander then got on his horse and set out for Strathmore to find that Paterson's works had been going on apace. Alexander went to his shepherd's house at Cashel Dhu where he penned a third letter to Mr Horsburgh at Tongue:

> On my way down Strathmore this morning I find that not only has the embankment referred to been put across the whole breadth of the water but that a new channel for the river has been commenced, and made considerable progress in, thro' a part of the best haugh we have on the Strath. So unwarranted a proceeding I have not met with. If you do not immediately stop this I shall tomorrow send an express for an Interdict from the Sheriff, to prevent which, I would humbly suggest your immediately coming to the spot, and I shall be happy to see you at Eriboll if you do. The bearer can describe what is doing, he being herded on the ground.[33]

The Cashel Dhu shepherd would be the bearer of this letter and he would have crossed the river, set out along the Moine path below the north face of Ben Hope, continued down to Kinloch and then on past Ribigill to Mr Horsburgh's house in Tongue. It is a distance of about twelve miles there and the same distance back again. They could walk in those days.

Unfortunately the correspondence in the estate records ends there. What was the outcome of all this? Today there is no dyke across the river, but then any average spate of that river would have cleared away long ago anything that stood in its path. The river still sweeps round the loop of the Luib Bhan, just as it has

---

33 National Library of Scotland, *Sutherland Collection.* I am very grateful to the late Mr Geoffey Baggott who found and passed on to me all the information describing the affair of the Luib Bhan.

1847.

NORTH
AND
WEST OF SUTHERLAND
FARMER CLUB.

THE following **PREMIUMS** will be awarded at **ALTNAHARROW**, on the first **TUESDAY** of **APRIL, 1847** :—

For the best PLAID, Shepherd's Pattern, ...	£0	12	0	For the best Pair of STOCK-INGS, ...	£0	5	0
For the Second best ditto,	0	8	0	For the Second best Pair of do.	0	3	0
For the Third best ditto,	0	5	0	For the Third best ditto,	0	2	0
For the best PLAID, any Pattern or Colour,	0	12	0	For the best Pair of SOCKS,	0	4	0
For the Second best ditto,	0	8	0	For the Second best ditto,	0	3	0
For the Third best ditto,	0	5	0	For the Third best ditto,	0	2	0

To the Person who shall produce for Competition, the greatest number of **PAIRS** of STOCKINGS, whether they gain Premiums or not, ...   £0 10 0

To the Person who shall produce for Competition, the greatest number of Pairs of SOCKS, ...   0 10 0

To the Person who shall appear in the best Entire SUIT (Coat, Waistcoat, and Trowsers), of NATIVE MANUFACTURE, ...   £1 0 0

To the Second best ditto, ...   0 10 0

The WOOL used in the manufacture must be Grown, Dyed, and Woven, in the district under the Tongue and Scowrie Managements, or in the Parishes of Lairg and Creich. Articles that have been shown for Competition on any former occasion, cannot be entered again for that purpose ; nor will it be permitted in competing for the greatest number of Pairs of Stockings, or Socks, that the Competitor shall purchase any such Stockings or Socks,—they must all be the manufacture of his or her family. It is recommended that the Plaids be about three-and-a-half yards long, including the fringe, with border at each end. All articles of native manufacture, whether entered for Competition or not, will be purchased at their proper value, if desired.

ALEX. CLARKE,
Hon. Secretary.

Printed at the John O'Groat Journal Office, Wick.

Poster advertising a competition for best shepherd's plaid and other garments.

done for a thousand years or more. However the faint trace of a channel or the remains of a filled-in channel can still be found across the Luib Bhan. Paterson must indeed have been persuaded to desist and he did make – or was forced to make – some attempt at restoring the Luib Bhan to its original state.

Why did Paterson attempt such an outrageous interference with a neighbour's land? Was there some conflict between the Patersons at Melness and the Clarkes at Eriboll? Both were large and desirable sheep farms. Melness was huge, around 70,000 acres, and probably the largest sheep farm in Sutherland. It stretched for more than fifteen miles from the south end of Ben Hope northwards to the sea at Whiten Head. Eriboll was about 35,000 acres but a better farm. Possibly Paterson thought that, as Alexander's father had died in February of that year, Alexander would have plenty on his hands and would not take any action. If so, he seriously misjudged Alexander. Alexander was not the man to allow his neighbour to get the better of him. Whatever the reason was for Paterson's extraordinary course of action, I have never heard of any farmer ever going on to his neighbour's farm and starting to dig a channel there without discussing it with them first.

The Farmer Club

Alexander also became the honorary secretary of the 'North and West of Sutherland Farmer Club'. This Club awarded premiums for the stockings and plaids which shepherds knitted while herding their flocks. On the first Tuesday of April 1847, there was a great gathering at Altnaharrow (Altnaharra) where the garments were judged and the following premiums awarded:

For the best PLAID, shepherd's pattern: 12/-
For the best pair of STOCKINGS: 5/-
For the best pair of SOCKS: 4/-

and additional prizes –

> For the person who shall produce the greatest number of pairs of stockings: 10/-
>
> For the person who shall produce the greatest number of pairs of socks: 10/-
>
> For the person who shall appear in the best entire suit: £1: 0: 0 (Coat, waistcoat and trowsers, all to be of NATIVE MANUFACTURE.)

The regulations were strict:

> The wool used in the manufacture must be Grown, Dyed, and Woven in the district under the Tongue and Scowrie managements, or in the Parishes of Lairg and Creich ... nor will it be permitted in competing for the greatest numbers of Pairs of Stockings or Socks, that the Competitor shall purchase any such Stockings or Socks – they must all be the manufacture of his or her family ... the Plaid shall be about three-and-a-half yards long, including the fringe, with border at each end.[34]

The event was timed for early April, well before the start of the lambing and to give the shepherds the opportunity to sell the products of their own and their family's work during the previous year. There would be no time later. Lambing, clipping, speaning, sales and smearing would fully occupy the next six months although the knitting would continue. Almost all shepherds knitted as they herded their flocks, although I have been told that some of the shepherds were not very good at turning the heels. The

---

34 National Library of Scotland, *Sutherland Collection*. Thanks are due to Dr Malcolm Bangor-Jones for supplying all the information on this competition and for the accompanying poster.

wool came from their pack sheep and was added to by collecting any fallen wool. The wives carded the wool and used the spinning wheel to get it ready for knitting.

Then on 18 September 1852, Robert Horsburgh, the factor, sent out a circular letter, which read:

> A proposal has been made at Aultnaharrow on 7th inst. That a piece of plate be presented to Mr Clarke for his services as Secretary of the North and West Sutherland Farmer Club.

Negotiations for Renewal of the Lease

After the nineteen-year lease had been signed and secured in 1834, Alexander set out to improve Eriboll. Seven years later he sent Mr Horsburgh, the factor, a list of the improvements that he wished to carry out on Eriboll. This was followed in 1847 by a statement which details the need to reclaim land so that more turnips could be grown and then a most detailed and extensive list of the improvements that had been carried out by the Clarkes on Eriboll since the commencement of the lease. The improvements on the Eriboll arable and surrounding lands were shown on an excellent map which Alexander had had prepared. In his report of 1832 Patrick Sellar had written that, 'The house at Eriboll is very frail' and a new farmhouse had been built by Alexander. This is shown on the site of the present lodge and, at some date in the future, Alexander's building must have been greatly enlarged to form the present Lodge. There were also four new shepherds' houses, additions to the farm steading, new dykes, a new cut and embankment for the river in Strabeg, trenching and clearing nineteen acres to make new arable land at Eriboll and much else. And, amongst all the other improvements, there was a meal mill which was well on its way to being established on the road to the shore. This was powered by a lade that carried the water from the pond in the middle of the arable fields. The small burns, which carried the water to this pond, had been straightened and deepened with benefit both to the drainage of the surrounding land and to the flow of water. When this mill was in operation, there must have been great rejoicing for it meant an end to the separation of the oats from the stalks by flailing the sheaves, the drying of the oats in the kiln and then the daily task of grinding the oats in a quern, carried out by the women on the farm. Particularly there was the cutting of some sixty-six miles of what he calls Surface Drains – and what we would call sheep drains. Fifty-eight miles of these were two feet wide and one foot deep while the remaining eight miles were three and a half feet wide and fifteen inches deep. These sixty-six miles of sheep drains are of particular interest. I have been told by the older generation of shepherds – and whose opinions I greatly respect – that it was sheep drains like these which did more to improve hill grazings than any other measure and thereby the sheep stock. In those first fourteen years of the lease an enormous amount of work had been carried out. The farm must have been a hive of activity with contractors building houses, drainers cutting drains and dykers building the drystone dykes. The only proposed item which was not carried out was the twenty acres of 'Lands for planting'. These were planned as shelter belts, which would have provided shelter against winds from north. An additional belt was planned which would have sheltered the steading, the farmhouse and the fields near at hand from the prevailing south west winds. One wonders if it was at this time that the broadleaved trees, which now shelter Eriboll, were planted. If so, it would make them almost a hundred and seventy years old at the present time and, indeed, they could well be just about as old as that.

On 15 October 1847, Alexander sent Robert Horsburgh, the factor, the following: 'Note of Money laid out on Eriboll Farm since Whitsunday 1834, the commencement of the present lease by Mr Clarke'. This reads:

New dwelling house		£589
Sheds at both ends of do with out house	35	£624
Road to the new House, from public road, cost		10
Strabeg Cut and Embankment for altering the course of the river upwards of 2000 yards in length, cost		£338
Building 2483 yards new Dykes at Eriboll, cost		160
4 New Shepherds Houses, cost		80
Additions to the farm steading, new Roofing & slating old dwelling house, cost		160
Fence round Sea Rocks at Huilem 656 yards, cost		9
Park at Strabeg, for hay &c &c, cost		20
Park at Arnaboll for Do, cost		10
Sheep Drains, about 65 Miles made, cost		130
Trenching, clearing and Draining 19 acres new Arable Lands made at Eriboll, cost		120
Total Sum expended		£1661

For part of the above outlays there is allowed by the Proprietor a deduction of £50 annually from the Rent, during the Lease, in all		£950
Cash received on finishing Strabeg Cut p(e)r agreement	60	£1010
Leaving Money already expended, over the sum to be ultimately paid		£651
To which add, the sum to be laid out over the allowance of £50 annually, now asked, for the improvements proposed, as above		150
Leaving the sum to be laid out by the tenant, without any remuneration from the Proprietor		£801

Besides the in[teres]t of £600 sunk in the Dwelling
House, for 16 years at 5 [e]r Cent, amounts to   £480.

Both sums   £1281[35]

This is a detailed and very complicated calculation which
Alexander has drawn up to show how much he was out of
pocket on these improvements despite the various deductions
on the rent made by the proprietor. It does seem that it was
Alexander who had paid for all these improvements and not
the estate. To anyone of my generation, who has tenanted land
under the terms of the 1947 Agricultural Act, this is most odd.
Under that Act it was the landlord who was responsible for
providing the fixed equipment on the farm and for maintain-
ing it. All the tenant had to do was to farm the land according
to the rules of good husbandry and pay the rent which could
be determined by arbitration. In practice the landlord seldom
provided the fixed equipment which the tenant thought was
necessary. However the principle was generally accepted that
the farm was the property of the landlord and therefore it was
he who should provide the fixed equipment and maintain it.
This was a most useful principle in negotiations over the lease
and the rent. Different times bring different customs. The fact
is that it was Alexander who paid for those improvements at
Eriboll and he clearly felt that the reductions in rent did not
compensate him adequately for his outlays.

The next question that must be asked is: 'Where did he get
the money to pay for all these improvements?' Certainly farming
was starting to recover from the serious slump in prices which
followed the end of the Napoleonic wars but it has also long
been understood within the family that Marion, Alexander's wife,
inherited a considerable sum of money around this time. If that
is so, then it must have been most gratefully received.

35 National Library of Scotland, *Sutherland Collection*. Again I am deeply indebted to Dr Malcolm Bangor-Jones for obtaining all this information for me.

In 1847, Alexander also wrote a dissertation to James Loch, the commissioner for the Sutherland Estates, on the need for the sheep farms in Sutherland to be provided with enough arable land on which to grow turnip. He maintained that this would increase the value of the sheep farms on the estate and hence they could be let for a higher rent. It would also mean that money, currently spent on away wintering in Easter Ross and the Black Isle, would remain within the county of Sutherland and would provide employment there. Loch was not enthusiastic and nor were his factors. Certainly it would mean a nice crop of turnip growing on every hill farm but it would be costly. The factors also saw that, not only would money have to be spent on reclaiming a suitable piece of moorland, but that further expenditure must then be incurred on stables for extra horses and on cottages for the ploughmen. After all, these horses and ploughmen would all need to be housed. The tenant could not grow turnip unless he had the horsepower and the manpower to do so. Further, if the tenant paid for the improvements, he would require to be given a rebate on his rent of 5% on the capital expended, or, if the estate paid for the improvements, then the tenant would have to be made to agree to an increase of 5% on the capital which would be spent by the estate for these improvements plus the extras.

In 1858 Alexander wrote out in detail his proposals for a new lease of Eriboll, which he sent to Mr Horsburgh, the factor. Reading through all these papers a hundred and fifty years later, it is clear that Alexander lacked neither energy, nor diligence, nor skill in preparing his case for a renewal of the lease at a favourable rent. Apart from the farming facts and figures he asks the factor to:

> Consider such a locality as I am placed in, not within 12 miles of any neighbour, 18 miles from Church, not within reach of any School for my Children, distant from a Post

Office and 60 miles from the nearest market Town. All these circumstances are uncomfortable, and render the keeping of a family at least 10 per Cent more expensive than a Situation differently situated.

He continues:

I am most anxious to continue a tenant under the Noble family of Sutherland, more especially as His Grace, The Duke of Sutherland, has kindly agreed to renew the Lease of the farm to me, and believing that an adequate Rent only is wished by His Grace, 'to live and let live' that I am most willing to give.

And, after all that, he concludes with a list of the expenses he will have to face, namely Poors (sic) Rates @ 1/- per £, Road money @ 4d per £, Schoolmasters Salary of £3: 6: 2 and Income Tax @ 2d per £1. In the end it was all well worth it for on 31 July 1852 the Duke signed a new lease for Eriboll for nineteen years.[36] Had Alexander not been satisfied with any of the conditions, he would certainly not have added his signature. He always drove a hard bargain. Alexander would not have reached the position he achieved, had he not done so.

Meddat

Alexander was a great flockmaster. In addition to Eriboll, his farming expanded and he took the tenancy of Meddat, an excellent large arable farm in the Easter Ross parish of Kildary. There he installed his eldest son, also Alexander (1829–1878). It was young Alexander's home for the rest of his life and the house

36 National Library of Scotland, *Sutherland Collection*. Once again I am indebted to Dr Malcolm Bangor-Jones for obtaining all this detailed information for me.

where, down the years, many members of the Clarke family were to spend time, particularly in the winter. My father and his brother, Rupert, were both born in the farmhouse there. Meddat was to play a key part in the successful management of the Eriboll flock, wintering the hoggs and supplying the needs of what Sellar graphically calls 'the weak end of the flock'. Certainly each year all the hoggs would have gone down there in September and then come back to Eriboll at the end of March. From the clipping list of 1833, there must have been at least 1,200 hoggs to winter – five hundred ewe hoggs and seven hundred wether hoggs. It would have been quite sight to see this flock, driven at a rate of eight to ten miles a day over the sixty-five miles from Eriboll, through Sutherland, over the Struie and down to Kildary, and then all the way back again in the spring. It was becoming common practice for the larger Sutherland hill farms to rent the wintering of a lowground arable farm for the hoggs from a tenant famer, but it was much better to lease the whole farm from the landlord. The flockmaster could then organise and crop the farm to suit the needs of the hoggs – at least as far as the seven-course rotation allowed him. That seven-course rotation was a wise system, commonly written into the lease of the farm. It meant that the farmer was required to crop the fields of the farm in a six or seven year rotation – lea oats, turnips, oats or barley undersown with grass followed by three or four years in grass. Thus 2/7th of the farm would be in grain (the only cash crop), 1/7th in turnips and 4/7th in grass. The grass would be cut for hay the first year and grazed for the other two or three years. During the summer there would be not be a single sheep on the farm, only cattle and horses. It was then clean for the hoggs when they arrived in September. This grazing system ensured that, by the fourth year in grass, a thick sward of wild white clover had developed. The ploughing in of this sward gave the land the fertility it required to carry it through its next three years of cropping, aided by the application of the dung from the cattle courts. This was carted out, spread on the lea oat stubble and ploughed in ready for the turnip crop. While a large proportion of the turnips would be clipped, carted in and fed to the cattle in the steading, the remainder would be eaten off by the hoggs, giving the land the blessing of the golden hoof. It was a most excellent system. It never varied. It made the land, it made the stock and it made the farmer.

As the price of wool and mutton increased, Eriboll was well placed to flourish. There was now a large, sound Cheviot ewe and wether stock while Meddat was there to carry the burden of the wintering. It is said that if hoggs get a good harvesting – that is the first six weeks of their wintering – then a good wintering will follow and the hoggs will come home each spring well wintered – year after year. Such husbandry will do much to build a flock of note and this is just what the combination of Eriboll and Meddat supplied. Alexander Clarke senior was a flockmaster well capable of directing the whole operation.

Life did not always go smoothly. In 1853 Alexander's son, George Granville, went to Durness and there recorded the birth of his son, James, in the Durness Register of Births and Deaths, 'N.B.L.W.' (Not Born in Lawful Wedlock) being neatly added after the entry. The mother of the child was Johan Macdonald (1831–1907) who lived at Polla with her father, who is said to have been the foxhunter. It is also said that Johan was working as a domestic servant in the farmhouse at Eriboll. However both families decided that Johan and George were too young to get married. The child was christened 'James Clarke' and Johan raised the boy, who was to become the progenitor of a fine race of Clarkes. Alexander was to see George married to Elizabeth Anne Sutherland Clarke, a distant cousin who had come back to Sutherland from Tasmania, and three children would be born to that marriage between 1860 and 1862.

Encroaching Deer

Shootings began to have an increasing financial value as sporting assets for the estate owner. They could now be let for a much higher rent than could ever be obtained from a sheep farmer. Conflict developed between landowner and flockmaster as to whether it was to be the sheep or the deer who were to graze the land. On the one hand there was the sporting tenant, the landowner and his forester (the stalker). On the other hand there was the flockmaster and his shepherds. All parties were most deeply involved. Each and all had their own interests to protect. As early as 1837 the Duke of Sutherland's forester on the Reay Forest, Hugh Mackenzie, was writing:

> I am well aware that the Sheep Farmers don't wish the Shepherds to poach or disturb Deer or Game of any kind, but when they are amongst the hills the temptation is so great that they cannot resist it, the consequence is, that they not only kill game, but also neglect their employer's interest – both the Proprietors and the Tenants are loosers [*sic*] by the liberty they have in carrying Guns.

In that same year there is a note in the Sutherland estate papers:

> Mr Clarke, Eriboll, is encroaching on the Forest [the Reay Forest] by pasturing Cattle and Sheep to Plataray [*Plat Reidh*] – the east end of Foinnivhein [Foinaven] about a score of each and a great many sheep. 2nd He has subset part of his farm to a man of the name of McDonald, the Southside of Glengolly [Glen Golly] following Ledneglish and Lurgugh Havel [*Lurg on t Sabhail*] to Ballichnafaign [*Bealach na Freithe*], who takes in Cattle to Grase [*sic*] in summer from individuals who carry guns and poach under the pretext that they are looking after their Cattle.

It does seem from this that Alexander and his father before him was or had been grazing on land that was to form part of what is now recognised as the Reay Forest. Certainly it has always been understood in the Clarke family that Eriboll sheep had grazed in the Reay Forest, whether officially or not, ever since John Clarke took the lease of Eriboll. This was now to end. The coming of the demand for deer stalking was to cause great changes in outlook. The factor and the forester required that there would now be no access by shepherds, for that would disturb the deer. The Eriboll sheep had long been accustomed to graze what was now strictly deer forest ground and the shepherds had to go in there to herd them. It follows that there was conflict between sporting tenant, briefed by the stalker, and the flockmaster. I would imagine that the correspondence, of which we have copies, is all that is left to tell of the argument which must have rolled back and forth. The area of the Reay Forest, which is indicated by the place-names given in the above note, would extend to some 20,000 acres and would contain some most useful grazing. Alexander would not have readily retreated from what he would have still regarded as 'his grazings'.

In 1850 Earl Grosvenor took a sporting lease from the Duke of Sutherland of the 'Lands of Foinabhin, Platory, Loan, and Arkle, which are formed into a Deer Forest lying in the Parishes of Edderachill and Durness'. Platory or Plataraeis (*Plat Reidh*) had been grazed as a part of Eriboll. In August of the same year Evander McIver, the factor, wrote to Alexander Clarke:

I have just had a note from Lord Anson from Loan Cottage – by which I find your Sheep are becoming troublesome to Lord Grosvenor's Forest – at the top of Meal Horn, Saval More and Saval Beg – whence they fall down on the Loan ground in hundreds. I have advised his Lordship Send Wm Ross [Forester] to you to explain his wishes. Be so good as direct your shepherds to keep your

Sheep within your own bounds – for I plainly see there will be disagreeable work if not – in the meantime I will see Lord Anson and do all in my power to preserve peace and keep him quiet.

Also in 1850 the shootings on Eriboll were let to a Mr C. M. Campbell from Shrewsbury for two seasons at a rent of £120 per annum: 'He is to find his own quarters as he best can and talks of an Iron room or a Road Caravan!'

Then in February 1852 Robert Horsburgh, the factor at Tongue, wrote to Evander McIver:

It would I think be very desireable, that one so respected as Mrs Scobie universally is should end her days in the Reay country, and I will be glad to learn that she determines to follow Mr Clarke's example by taking a new lease of her farm [Keoldale?] on the terms demanded. It has now become generally known that Mr Clarke is to remain at Eriboll, and a draft lease will be immediately prepared.

McIver suggested that a strict clause covering the straying of sheep be included in the new lease but Horsburgh did not want such a clause: 'It is by no means unlikely that the Sheep withdrawn from Platarae [*Plat Reidh*] would for a time be troublesome to Lord Grosvenor; but this will of course soon come to an end . . .' He added that there was no such clause in any other lease: 'I do not think it would be wise to add to the unpopularity of the Deer Forest system by now introducing them [i.e. such clauses], particularly as the sportsmen can, like other occupiers, so easily protect themselves at Common Law'.

In 1855 Alexander Clarke was himself granted the lease of the shootings on Eriboll for a rent of £40 on a quite separate agreement from his tenancy of the farm of Eriboll itself. Alexander knew what he was doing. He was determined to be able to protect his grazings at the south end of Eriboll from deer coming in from the Reay Forest and also take in some money from sporting tenants wishing to shoot grouse. With the growth of deer forests and the leasing of them to sporting tenants from the south, deer numbers were rising. Away back in 1838 Scrope had written that the Dirriemore, which was the place-name given to a great area of north-west Sutherland, was carrying some 1,200 deer. By 1852 the number of deer had increased greatly on this ground and especially in the Reay Forest. That deer forest seems to have been smaller in extent than when it had been originally owned by Lord Reay or when later it was owned by Lord Grosvenor (later the Duke of Westminster) but it was now carrying more deer. It was let to Mr Charteris (later Lord Elcho) along with the lodge at Gobernuisgach. This had been built by the Duke of Sutherland in 1846. Mr Charteris also wanted a part of Eriboll, probably the Glen Golly and Strabeg end, but Alexander Clarke firmly refused to give up the lease of any part of Eriboll whatsoever.

Four years later in 1856, George Loch, the commissioner, wrote to Evander McIver:

Lord Grosvenor has been with me a long time today – There are various Circumstances that make it undesirable for him to Continue, for the present, the large annual outlay connected with Stack – at the same time he is very reluctant to give it up. His wish would be, if possible, to retain the Shooting and the Laxford, and to find tenants who would, for the next three years, take it from year to year. He thinks the £360 p[er] ann: he pays for the forest quite as much as it is worth, that the ground near Fionbihin [sic], and Arkle is sterile and unfrequented by deer – and that the good proportion of his ground is where he approaches Sandy Clarke's march, and that here the deer are much disturbed by the Shepherds, and are Consequently driven into the Reay Forest – he tells me that he has, with his friends, killed a surprisingly Small number of Deer during the last two or three years, that in fact they are not to be had – on the other hand, he thinks the rent for the Laxford decidedly too low. He tells me that the whole thing 'stands him in £600 a yr.'[37]

In the above letter the voice of the head stalker on the Reay Forest can be heard pouring into Lord Grosvenor's ear – and to anyone else who would listen – on every possible occasion the terrible problems he was having with the Eriboll shepherds. This conflict was going to continue unabated down the years and still does. At that moment in time Alexander had had the foresight to get the tenancy of the shootings of Eriboll into his own hands. He and his sons or his sporting tenants could not be stopped shooting any deer that came on to the Eriboll ground.

The money from sporting lets to wealthy, aristocratic sportsmen from the south was to form a greater and greater proportion of estate income in the years to come. Rich sportsmen were and still are prepared to spend huge sums of money on equipping northern estates with all the requirements for a comfortable and successful stay during the season. As a consequence lodges, houses for the stalkers and bothies for the watchers were constructed, access paths into the forests were built and much employment was created, all so that many deer and grouse could be shot and great numbers of salmon and trout caught. Deer were – and still are – regarded as strictly private property by landowners and their sporting tenants, even when those deer have strayed out of the deer forest. The taking of deer by any other party anywhere and at any time was – and still is – utterly condemned by landowners though it may only be a crofter trying to protect his crops from raiding deer. Slowly and unwillingly the flockmasters had to give way before the power of this wealth. More and more land was

37 Letter from Dr Malcolm Bangor-Jones giving me this information from his work on the history of the Reay Forest.

turned over to deer forests. In the case of Eriboll, an occasional deer would go on being taken by the shepherds on the hirsels marching with the Reay Forest. After all it was the sheep's meat that the deer were taking.

There is also a record in the Sutherland papers of a proposal in 1858 for a 'Huge colonization scheme at Eriboll' but Alexander would right away put the death wish on that project. There is no further mention of it.

There is an interesting sidelight on Alexander in Hew Morrison's record of his time as teacher to seventeen pupils at Eriboll around 1866. He writes: 'It was old Mr Clarke [Alexander] who paid me my salary of £2 per quarter – £8 per annum plus free board and lodging. These two items were supplied free of charge by the shepherds with whom he stayed. While not over-generous, it was a reasonable salary for a young teacher in those days.' The church, which had been built alongside the road half a mile north of Eriboll in 1804, was used for the school. That church is marked as the Free Church on the first Ordnance Survey of 1874 and has been most carefully restored by the present owner of Eriboll. Hew Morrison also records conversations with Alexander on matters of Clarke genealogy and family history. It seems that Hew Morrison and Alexander Clarke were distantly related.[38]

On 28 August 1877 Alexander died at Rosemount near Tain. He was seventy-five years of age. His widow, Marion, lived on after him for another nine years. She died, again at Rosemount, on 7 January 1886. She was eighty-six years of age. They had been married for fifty years, had reared a family of eight children, five boys and three girls all born within the space of thirteen years. All the children were doing well. Alexander, his eldest son, was farming Meddat very successfully and was a respected member of the Easter Ross farming community; John was a surgeon in the army, attached to the 13th Light Infantry; George Granville was farming Eriboll. He had married his cousin, Elizabeth Anne

38 Article in *Am Bratach*, September 2009, 'Hew Morrison of Skerray'.

Clarke, from Tasmania, who had died in 1870 just after the birth of their third child. The three children from that marriage were now teenagers and George had married again. David was a captain in Bengal Staff Corps in India and Eric Donald had emigrated to New Zealand. Of the girls Johanna had died when only four years old, Janet had stayed at Eriboll and was tutor to Alexander's grandchildren and Jemima did not marry either. Alexander could look back on a lifetime of successful pastoral farming and a steady accumulation of wealth. He had overcome many difficulties. He had risen to become one of the most respected flockmasters in the county of Sutherland, and had been a Deputy Lord Lieutenant and a Justice of the Peace for that county.

It was thanks to the sheep that all this had been achieved. The following inscription was engraved in 1485 on a window pane by one Master John Barton, flockmaster and wool merchant, Squire of Holme, near Newark in the far away county of Nottingham.

> I thanke God and ever shall,
> It is the shepe that payeth for all.

That inscription was once true of the Sutherland sheep farms and their flockmasters. It was especially true of Alexander Clarke.

9

George Granville Leveson-Gower Clarke (1833–1904)

Born at Eriboll, 28 November 1833. Flockmaster at Eriboll. Also farmed Meddat, near Kildary, and Rosemount, near Tain. Justice of the Peace for the County of Sutherland. Died in a nursing home in Edinburgh, 26 June 1904, aged seventy-one years.

Children

By Johan Macdonald who was born at Polla, Loch Eriboll c. 1831, died 1907, a son, James Clarke, born 1853 (illegitimate), died at Kempie, 1921.

Married (1) Elizabeth Anne Sutherland, born at Glen Dhu on the Ouse, Tasmania, 2 May 1839, died at Meddat, Kildary, 12 June 1870, aged thirty-one years.

George, born c. 1866.

Huttie, born c. 1868.

John (Jack), Charles, born c. 1870, died in South Africa c. 1940.

(2) Sophie Jane Walter, born at Langton Rectory, Horncastle, Lincolnshire, 2 March 1834, died at Eriboll, 1 November 1884, aged fifty years. No children.

(3) Alice Gibson, born in the parish of Brent with Furneaux Pelham, Hertfordshire, 1845, died at Nigg, Easter Ross, 1927, aged eighty-two.

Reay Falconer, born at Meddat 1890, died at Edderton 1931, aged forty-one years.

Rupert Henry, born at Meddat 1892, died at Eriboll 3 June 1920, aged twenty-eight years.

George Granville Leveson-Gower Clarke was born at Eriboll on 28 November 1833, the third child in a family of eight children; five boys and three girls. He was given his many names in honour of his father's landlord and patron, George Granville Leveson-Gower, 1st Duke of Sutherland, who had died in July of that year.

George Granville was brought up at Eriboll and was probably taught – and well taught – by a tutor. George was an excellent shot with both rifle and shotgun. While growing up at Eriboll George Granville certainly had the opportunity and encouragement to acquire that skill. He joined the Highland Rifle Militia, a forerunner of the Territorial Army, and gained his commission. There are two pewter tankards in the possession of our family. One of these is inscribed as follows:

WON BY Lt G. G. Clarke. H. R. Militia [Highland Rifle Militia]
From: Lt Col Ross, Capt Houston, Lt Smith and Mr Maclennan, H. R. Militia, Lt Crane, 72nd Highlanders and Ens Drysdale, 93rd Highlanders.
FORT GEORGE. 3:5:61.

George Granville would then have been twenty-eight years old. The second tankard is not inscribed, though otherwise similar. George was indeed a good shot – a better shot than his commanding officer, Lieutenant Colonel Ross of Cromarty.

There is also a group photo of the officers of the Highland Rifle Militia taken outside the Mess at Fort George. It is a group of very worthy officers, many of whose family names are still represented in the north. George Granville stands at the left end of the back row.

Around the year 1860 he married his second cousin, Elizabeth Anne Clarke (1839–1870), the daughter of James Clarke (1791–1853) and granddaughter of Charles Clarke of Glendhu. James had emigrated to Tasmania in 1825 and had there created a fine property which he called Glen Dhu, after the old home in Sutherland. Elizabeth had been born in Tasmania and James had left money in his will for her to return to Scotland. She must have travelled up to Sutherland to see her father's late home – Glendhu, up the loch from Kylesku – and meet her relatives, including George Granville. They fell in love and they married. He was about thirty and she was twenty-one. They had three children in the space of their four or five years of marriage. She died at Meddat in 1870 and is buried in Balnakiel churchyard. She was only thirty-one. George was left a widower with his three young children.

George then married Sophia Jane Walter, a clergyman's daughter from Langton, Horncastle in Lincolnshire, who was in her early forties. She must have been fully occupied bringing up George's three teenage children. She is listed in the 1881 census as being forty-six years of age, the wife of George Granville, and they were all staying with his mother, Marion Clarke, at their farm of Rosemount near Tain. The same census lists George as farming a total of 40,000 acres, eight hundred acres being arable, and employing forty men and from ten to forty women. It was a big handling. Jane and he had no children and she died at Eriboll in 1884, when she would have been fifty. She also is buried in Balnakiel Cemetery.

In 1889 George Granville married Alice Gibson, again a clergyman's daughter and this time from Brent Pelham in Hertfordshire where her father was the vicar. Alice Gibson was a woman of strong character. Her mother was a Hubbard. The Hubbard family were very successful London merchants trading with Russia. They had a house, offices and warehouses in St Petersburg. Alice went out there in 1873 and spent almost a year with the family. It is clear from her letters home that she enjoyed a busy social life with picnics, sleigh rides and dances.

It is a fair question to ask how Alice Gibson, the daughter of an English vicar, ever came to meet, to fall in love with and to marry this Highland flockmaster from the northern extremity of the United Kingdom. It is said that George Granville suffered from a number of minor illnesses and complaints, although these never stopped him from farming successfully. It has also been said that he went to Bath and elsewhere in search of a cure. Maybe it was in Bath, taking the waters, that they met. He was seventeen years older than Alice but fall in love and marry they did. George took his bride north where she established herself as mistress of Eriboll for the next thirty years. She loved Eriboll.

Their first son, Reay Falconer, my father, was born in 1890 and then Rupert Henry in 1892. By this time Alice was forty-five years of age and George was fifty-nine, an elderly couple to be starting a family. Rupert, my uncle, was born with Down's Syndrome. He was to die at Eriboll at the age of twenty-eight, having spent his life there and at Meddat and having been much loved by all.

George Granville, with his payroll of forty men and ten to forty women, was reckoned to be a good employer. It is told that, before a Lairg sale, he used to give his head shepherd, Donald Mackay, two guineas with which to pay any expenses in the way of meals and board incurred by the Eriboll shepherds on their journey there with the lambs, while at the sale itself and during the walk back. When he got back to Eriboll after the sale, Donald had to report to Mr Clarke, give an account of how the money had been spent and hand over the change. One year Donald failed to appear and was sent for. A very embarrassed Donald duly arrived. On being asked to explain what had happened, how the money had been spent and why the change had not been handed over, Donald said something like this:

Well sir, I am afraid that there is an unfortunate habit for shepherds to gather in the bar at Lairg after the sale and discuss all that has been going on since they last met. And, of course, Sir, I had to go there as well to make sure that all was in order. Now, this year, in that bar, the question arose as to who had the best master in Sutherland. And one said that he had the best master for was not a pair of horse sent up to plough the tattie ground for him when there was all that trouble at the lambing. And another said 'No, he had the best master in Sutherland for, when the thatch on his house was blown off in that bad gale, didn't his boss get on to the factor right away and my roof was secured with new corrugated iron before the winter's gales started'. Oh, Mr Clarke! I could not let that go. What was there for me to do but to climb up on the table and shout 'Now look, boys, just be quiet! You are all wrong! It is us from Eriboll that has the best master in Sutherland, for didn't Mr Clarke give me these two guineas to buy you all drink!' There was a cheer and that was where the two guineas went. And, oh Mr Clarke, I am afraid there was no change.

To which George Granville replied: 'Donald, I do understand what happened but this must never be allowed to occur again,' and that was the end of the matter.[39]

George Granville appears to have been as keen on improving Eriboll as his father had been. However in Alexander's time it was he who carried out and paid for the improvements, being granted remission on the rent to the value of the interest on the cost of these improvements, or at least on some of them; now it was the other way round. George Granville carried out and paid for the improvements but the estate either reimbursed him for his expenditure or paid the contractor directly and then charged him interest as an addition to the rent. For the period between 1872

39 Told to me by the late P. D. Robertson, Castlecraig.

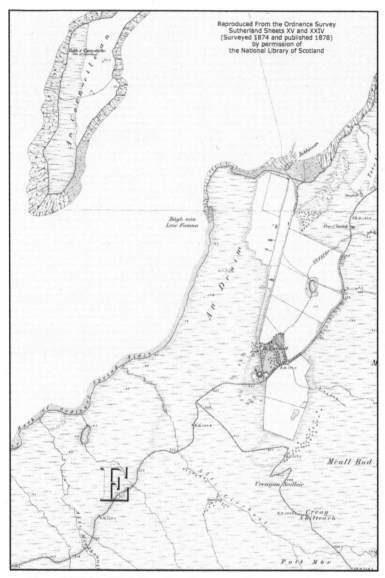

Reproduced From the Ordnance Survey
Sutherland Sheets XV and XXIV
(Surveyed 1874 and published 1878)
by permission of
the National Library of Scotland

The arable fields of Eriboll, perhaps showing trenching in progress, c. 1873.

and 1878, there is a long list of expenditure for improvements to the farm steading, to servants' cottages, to new shepherds' houses and also repairs to other houses, to repairing the dykes of the shepherds' parks at Heilem, Strabeg and Arnaboll and additional works. However one of the main items is the sum of £2800 spent on land improvements. It seems that this must have been the cost of the trenching, cultivating and the clearing of stones on what are now the fields that rise from the road to the shore plus the two fields below the church – maybe seventy-five to eighty acres in all. They would also have received lime and dung and been carefully farmed with a rotation of crops. Today the green sward on those fields bears testimony to the care and diligence of the cultivators. It also bears witness to the labour of the women of Laid, who came across the loch each morning and gathered the stones which now lie in great heaps beside the road to the shore. The first Ordnance Survey of c. 1874 seems to show that work actually in progress. There are three distinct steps shown on the map of that hillside and appear to record the work as it was being done. It does seem that three men were engaged in trenching that hillside on the very day that the Ordnance surveyors were carrying out their survey on Eriboll.

Eriboll was the heart of George Granville's farming enterprise but there were also the two arable farms in Easter Ross, Meddat and Rosemount. These gave support by wintering the hoggs and 'the weak end of the flock'. Meddat near Kildary is a fine arable farm and Alexander, George's elder brother, was the tenant there until he died. George Granville then took on the tenancy. My father, Reay Falconer Clarke, was born in Meddat farmhouse in 1890. Rosemount, near Tain, was a smaller Easter Ross farm where the family often went for the winter. The coming of the railway to Lairg in the 1860/70s must have greatly eased the transport problem of getting down to Easter Ross and back again. However there were still the sixty or so miles to cover from Lairg to Eriboll in the horse-drawn carriage driven by John Gunn, for many years the coachman at Eriboll. It is a long road from Lairg up to the Crask, through Strath Vagastie to Altnahara, past Mudale and down into Strathmore. At the bottom end of Strathmore and almost at the south end of Loch Hope is Cashel Dhu. There was a ford or a ferry there across the river. Then it was up over the Eriboll ground by the road known as the Creagan and down to Eriboll itself. However, if the river was up and not passable, it was north along the east side of Loch Hope to the Hope River which could now be crossed thanks to the Duke of Sutherland's chain ferry. This carried coach, horses and passengers safely across without the horses being unyoked. Then it was up to Heilam, on past Kempie and then alongside the loch to Eriboll. It was a long drive and the horses would need to have been well rested in Lairg the previous night so that they would be fit for that long and arduous journey.

At that time there would have been a large community at Eriboll. At Eriboll itself there would have been a grieve, a cattle-man and two ploughmen to work the now increased arable land and to assist at the handlings plus their wives and families. Then there would have been shepherds and their families at Heilam, Arnaboll, two at Cashel Dhu, herding the two hirsels there, and probably one family with two shepherds herding the double herding at Strabeg. There was also a shepherd and his family at Polla with, finally, the head shepherd at Eriboll itself. Each of these shepherds would often have had a boy to help him with his herding. Extra help was taken on in spring to help with the lambing, marking and clipping. I have been told that, when a lad came applying for a post at the lambing at Eriboll, it was only if he came from Skye that George Granville would give him the job. It makes a total of perhaps as many as fifty or more people living and working there; four at the farm; then eight shepherds, plus maybe half a dozen boys; plus those taken on for the lamb-ing; plus all the wives and families. On top of that there would have been one or perhaps two hogg shepherds who had been looking after the stock that had been wintered down at Meddat and Rosemount. These may well have stayed on at Eriboll when they arrived back with the hoggs in the spring and then helped with the lambing and clipping. And, in addition to all these, there were of course George Granville's own family and domestic staff in the farmhouse. Eriboll was well staffed, well run and the sheep were indeed well herded.

George Granville was a noted flockmaster, a respected judge of sheep and an able farmer. His men stayed with him. It is said that the Campbell family herded the Arnaboll hirsel on the side of Loch Hope for some seventy years and through three generations. George Granville was indeed reckoned to be a good employer. Many years ago I met Joseph Mackay, who was then the wintering shepherd in Edderton for Abner Anderson. Mr Anderson rented a number of farms and crofts for wintering hoggs in Easter Ross. Before coming to Edderton Joseph had herded on Eriboll. He told me that George Granville was much respected by all for his great knowledge of sheep and for the fact that he would always stop his carriage if he saw shepherds working at a fank or stell and make his way down to see how the sheep were looking and how the work was going.

A new lease was agreed in 1872 and this time it would appear to have been Evander Maciver, the Scourie factor, who conducted most of the negotiations. There seems to have been an acceptance that it was the proprietor who would carry out the repairs and improvements to the buildings. Almost £3000 was spent on carrying these out. The estate also paid £603:19: 2 for 'new farm road, mill lead race & sluice and roadside drains and sundry works'. Then there was £2800 for 'Expenditure on Reclamations' but here the tenant was to pay interest at 2.5% annually on this sum as part of his rent. Clearly the drive to carry out improvements on Eriboll was there with George Granville as it had been with his father, Alexander. The enthusiasm for reclaiming land had been led by the Duke of Sutherland himself, although maybe this attitude was not fully shared by his factors. They had to keep track of all the money expended. And perhaps also, by this time or a little later, the Duke himself was not as keen as he had been, for there is a note that in March 1878 the steam engines which had been carrying out the reclamations on Ribigill near Tongue were to be sent back to Trentham. George Granville was also able to secure a separate and further lease of the shootings over Eriboll plus angling on the Polla River and a boat on Loch Hope.[40]

Eriboll was a good and well-equipped farm. The assessment for rates which was carried out in 1914 gives a most detailed account of the buildings, as do the sale particulars drawn up by the estate agents, Knight, Frank and Rutley, in 1919. By that time the owner was William Ewing Gilmour of Rosehall. George Granville would have been dead for some fifteen years but the buildings would not have altered much. This assessment lists Eriboll as a grazing farm of 31,069 acres, two roods, twelve poles and no square yards, let at a yearly rent of £502: 8: 3. The sale particulars add that the farm was let at a very low rent and that the lease was due to expire at Whitsun 1921. The shootings were also leased by the Clarkes, on a separate tenancy from the farm, for the sum of £195 paid annually.

Around 1840 Alexander had built his farmhouse on the site of what, in the Valuation Roll of 1914, is described as a 'Mansion House'. That house has been commonly called 'The Lodge' and is described as 'Eriboll Lodge' in the sale particulars for the Eriboll Estate in 1983. These sale particulars also state that it was formerly a shooting lodge for the Duke of Sutherland. It is listed as having three floors and some twenty rooms. These included a dining room and drawing room, a range of four bedrooms

40 National Library of Scotland, *Sutherland Collection*. Once again I have to thank Dr Malcolm Bangor-Jones for finding and sending me this information. I alone am wholly responsible for the conclusions which I have drawn both here and elsewhere.

with one W.C. lavatory, four attic bedrooms as well as a kitchen, butler's pantry, servants' hall and gun room. There is also a three stall stable and coach house, a keeper's house, a ghillies' bothy, and a housekeeper's house. Who carried out these developments? Was it the Clarkes who now held the sporting lease of Eriboll as well as, and separate from, the farm lease? Or was it the Duke of Sutherland? Whoever it was who carried out what appear to be enlargements and improvements to Alexander's original building and who also built the keeper's house and so on, most clearly designed the whole as a shooting lodge complex. It was in this lodge that the Clarkes certainly lived as a family at the end of George Granville's life and during the sixteen years that his widow was to live there. In 1869 Eriboll was listed in *The Sportsman's and Tourist's Guide* as yielding an annual bag of four hundred brace of grouse and six stags with excellent fishing in addition. How many brace of grouse are there on Eriboll today? The rating assessment of 1914 continues with ploughmen's cottages and, in the steading, a manager's house, a cart shed, a clipping shed, a mill and much else besides. All the buildings were stone and lime built with slated roofs. Then there were the five shepherd's houses with nearby byres and barns at Cashel Dhu, Arnaboll, Strabeg, Polla and Heilam. It was clearly a well-equipped farm.

Peter Stewart who lived in Laid at one time told a friend of mine, the late Geoffrey Baggott, how he remembered 'a big stackyard with dozens and dozens of haystacks, [and] cornstacks, higher than anything I've seen. They never had to buy anything (on the farm). They would sell potatoes and turnips.' He pointed out to me, across the loch from his window in Laid, where the water-driven threshing machine used to be. 'They turned the water on when they were going to thresh and you could see the thing come foaming down the hill [the rush of water coming down the mill lade]'. The traces of that mill lade are still there. This lade started at a sluice in a loch high up near the Creagan and descended down the steep brae face, across the fields and on to the steading. There the water drove a water-wheel, the power source for the threshing mill.[41]

The husbandry of the herding of hill sheep reached its peak on Eriboll at this time. The careful herding of each hirsel, the discipline of the regular ages of the ewe stock and the sound wintering of the hoggs down at Meddat all combined to build an outstanding sheep stock on Eriboll. The ewes were lifted off the greens at the same time every afternoon and would wend their way upwards to spend the night on the higher ground. It is a fine sight to see a heft of ewes and lambs in single file, untroubled and unhurried, climbing up from the lower grazings each evening. On the higher ground they would add the roughage of heather and bents to the grass already in their stomachs. Together these formed an ideal mixture on which to chew the cud and rest. In the morning the shepherd would walk the tops and turn the sheep back down onto the lower ground. The flockmaster could see that the shepherd was doing his work by the fresh state of the sheep paths which were always hard trodden from this daily and constant traffic. The lifting of the ewes from the greens every afternoon was the first rule in hill herding and formed a measure of pasture control. There were no fences in that countryside to control how and when the pastures were to be grazed but there were diligent shepherds who took a pride in the herding of their hirsels. It was rare for a shepherd to be inside his house during the hours of daylight – or as Patrick Sellar wrote: 'The shepherd's wages, however, much exceed those given to ploughmen. If a shepherd does his duty, he must exercise a great deal of consideration, and undergo much hardship; to which the man whose sleep is soundest in the wildest storm, and whose meat is regularly placed before him at certain hours is not subjected.'[42]

George Granville was also regularly employed as a valuer at waygoings. In 1890 he acted for the Duke of Sutherland at the

41 Letter from the late Geoffrey Baggott.
42 Patrick Sellar, *Farm Reports III. County of Sutherland*, Library of Useful Knowledge, 1831.

valuation of the sheep stock on Melness. The estate wished to end the sheep-farming tenancy on the high ground – the Ben Hope end of the farm – so that a deer forest could be established there with the prospect of a much higher rent. The northern and lower end of the farm was to be re-let as a sheep farm. The whole farm had been some 70,000 acres and had been herded in eight hirsels, only two of these being ewe hirsels. The farming tenant was clearly not unwilling to go along with this proposal. The herding of wethers on the high Ben Hope ground – largely for their wool – was no longer profitable due to the import of wool from Australia and elsewhere. Also the large joints of mutton from these big three and four-year-old wethers were being displaced by small joints of lamb imported from New Zealand. The outgoing tenant was William Mackay, and Donald Innes of Sandside acted for him at the valuation. The incoming tenant was the proprietor, the Duke of Sutherland, and George Granville Clarke acted for him. John Miller of Scrabster acted as oversman. It was a big valuation. When Donald Mackay had entered into the lease in 1866, he had taken over 1,772 ewes and 3,582 eild sheep – a total count of 5,354 sheep. That count is likely to have been about the same at the 1890 waygoing.[43]

There is an account in the *Northern Times* of 8 August 1901 of a communion service held on the shores of Loch Eriboll, almost certainly at Kempie.

> There was a congregation of between two and three hundred. The service was conducted in Gaelic by Mr Gunn, the minster of Durness, and in English by Mr Stewart, the minister of Rutherford. They preached from a tent improvised out of two oars and a sail, erected among the ferns at the base of the hill. The weather was exquisite. The plaintive singing of the psalms wafted over the heath.

43 Geoffrey Baggott. *Melness Farm, Sutherland: The Land Question and the Congested Districts Board.* Journal of Scottish Historical Studies 30th January 2010.

There was something exceedingly impressive in the scene when young and old, the rich and the poor, the Saxon and the Celt, reverently took their seats at the snow-white table under the open sky. One incident that added to the sweetness of the service was that, on the Monday afternoon, Mr Clarke, the farmer at Eriboll, had sent his carriage and pair to convey the old men and women of Melness near their homes.[44]

Telling of Kempie, let us go back to George Granville's first born son – James Clarke (*c.* 1853–1921). He grew up at Polla at the south end of Loch Eriboll and then went south to work on the railway at Lennoxtown. There he met and married Mary Couburgh (1856–1936). They had a family of three boys and five girls, the first three being born in Glasgow, the next five at Ardneackie on Loch Eriboll. There is a most interesting story behind that family's move from Ardneackie to Kempie and the building of their house there. Around 1891 it was decided to build a lighthouse on the eastern shores of Loch Eriboll and on 15 September 1894 James Clarke senior was appointed its first attendant. About the same time an arrangement had been made with the Sutherland Estate to allow him to build a house on Eriboll ground at Kempie. James set to and did just that. He even built a small window into one of the walls of Kempie from which a watch could be kept on the light. It all fitted a pattern. The new lighthouse needed a keeper, that keeper needed somewhere near the light to live and James was just the man to look after the light and build that house. And there is a further factor. A daughter had been born to James and Mary in 1893 and she was christened Georgina Alice Gibson. One wonders why those names were chosen. Were they chosen as a thank you and a compliment to George Granville's wife, Alice Gibson, whom George had married some three years before? Is it possible that Alice said to George

44 *Northern Times*, 8 August 1901.

Granville something like this: 'George, we are now both happily settled down at Eriboll and your son, Reay, is doing well. However your very first child, James, and his growing family are living in that crowded house at Ardneackie. Why don't you go and see the factor and arrange for James to be allowed to build himself a house at Kempie to be near the new lighthouse for he is likely to be appointed its keeper?' This is only a wild guess but for some reason James and Mary must have been very grateful to Alice to call their sixth child after Alice Gibson. Anyway James did build Kempie and he built it well. He and his wife reared their family of eight children there but in 1919 he took ill. His youngest son, James (1898–1976), was then serving with the Royal Navy but, at the request of the lighthouse service, he was released, came home and was appointed keeper of the light on 1 March 1919. James junior held that position for forty-four years and retired on 30 June 1963 when his son, Walter, took over. During those forty years James junior and his wife, Johan, reared a fine family of seven children, three sons and four daughters. Of these John and Walter continued to live at Kempie. Walter kept the light burning in the Loch Eriboll lighthouse until the Northern Lighthouse Board decided to close it down and demolished it in the 1960s.[45] John and Walter very successfully pursued their trade as fishermen. In 1996 they were able to buy Kempie and the attached garden from the Eriboll estate. A few years later they bought a house in Durness and moved there, handing Kempie over to their niece, Fiona Burnett, who lives there with her husband and daughter.

The late 1870s and the 1880s were financially depressing years for farming. The prices for wool and mutton collapsed. The grazings of the sheep farms were also showing signs of going back. It is worth quoting John R. Allan. He writes:

The hoof of the sheep was golden – for a while, but the land began to miss the crofter's cow and the crofter's wife.

45 Family Records and help from Mrs Mary Morrison.

By 1877 James Macdonald, special reporter of *The Scotsman* in Aberdeen (an agricultural reporter whose descriptions of the northern counties in the *Transactions* of the Highland and Agricultural Society are of the greatest value to anyone who wishes to understand why things are the way they are today), put it so: '[Some sheep farmers] are beginning to find that their farms will not carry so many sheep or keep them in so high condition as 15 or 20 years ago. Considerable portions of the grazings are becoming foggy and rough and of little value as sheep pasture. We could point to one or two hirsels which carried stocks of from 1,000 to 1,100 over winter some twenty years ago and which will now scarcely winter 800. The cause of this, we believe, is the covering of the land for so long a period exclusively by sheep, without any cattle being allowed on it. The experienced sheep farmer says, 'The land is getting tired of sheep and is needing to be cropped and thereby sweetened by highland cattle.' That is what the experienced sheep farmer is saying today as if he had newly discovered the fact.[46]

Flockmasters were faced with a serious struggle but George Granville survived. The estate had to grant some reductions in rents – rents which had been agreed when times were prosperous. George Granville is on record as applying for a form of rent reduction in that he might be excused paying the interest, which he was due to pay each year, on the capital which had been injected into Eriboll by the estate, largely for land reclamation. This appears to have been granted.

George Granville died on 26 June 1904 in a nursing home in Edinburgh. The press report in the *Highland News* of 2 July of that year states:

---

46 John R. Allan, *North-East Lowlands of Scotland*, 1952.

Many in the North will regret to hear of the death at Edinburgh a few days ago of Major George G. Clark of Eriboll. Deceased, who was 71 years of age, was one of the most extensive sheep farmers in Sutherland. A gentleman of kind and genial disposition, he was held in the highest respect by all classes of the community. He is survived by Mrs Clark and family, to whom much sympathy is extended. The funeral took place from Eriboll to Durness yesterday.[47]

Indeed George Granville was a respected figure. In a family photograph, taken around 1900, he appears tall with a large moustache, well dressed in a good tweed suit, stick in hand – a genial, friendly paterfamilias, yet with an air of command and determination about him. As reported in the *Highland News* he was buried at Balnakiel. A small plain headstone marks his grave on which the date of his death is incorrectly stated as 1909. Alongside him are buried his first two wives – Elizabeth Anne, mother of his first three children, and   his second wife, Jane Sophie. Their grave is marked by a plain headstone containing their names and the details of their births and deaths.

47 *Highland News*, 2 July 1904.

10

Alice Gibson Clarke (1845–1928)

Born at: Brent with Furneaux Pelham, Herts., 1845. Married George Granville Clarke (1833–1904) in 1888 (third wife). Died at 'The Whins', Nigg, Easter Ross, 1928, aged eighty-two years.

Children

Reay Falconer, born at Meddat 1890, died at Edderton, July 1931, aged forty-one.

Rupert Henry, born at Meddat 1892, died at Eriboll, 3 June 1920, aged twenty-eight.

Alice Gibson was born in the vicarage of Brent with Furneaux Pulham where her father Reverend John Gibson (1802–1863) was vicar for twenty-seven years. She was one of a family of thirteen children, four boys and nine girls. Her mother's family were Hubbards, who had founded the firm of John Hubbard and Company in 1771. This company traded very successfully with Russia from a head office in London. They had offices and warehouses in St Petersburg, exporting tallow, hemp, flax and grain to England and importing lead and tin to Russia. They also imported machinery and set up factories for spinning and weaving in Russia. Alice went out there and stayed with her brother, Bernard, for nine months in 1873–4 where she thoroughly enjoyed a busy social life with supper parties, balls, picnics and sleigh rides. On 23 January 1874 at the Winter Palace in St Petersburg she attended the wedding of Queen Victoria's second son, Alfred, Duke of Edinburgh, to the Grand Duchess Maria Alexandrovna of Russia, second daughter of Emperor Alexander II, Tsar of Russia. She describes all these and more in her excellent letters home. Alice came back to England in March 1874.[48]

Where and how Alice and George met we do not know. George Granville is known to have travelled to Bath and elsewhere to take the waters and, maybe, Alice and her father and mother went there as well. However George Granville did meet and marry Alice Gibson. George brought his bride to Eriboll and there she lived very happily for the next thirty-three years, usually spending the summers at Eriboll and part of the winters down in Easter Ross. George still held the tenancy of the farm of Meddat in Easter Ross and it was there that Reay Falconer, my father, was born in 1890. His brother, Rupert, was also born there two years later. As already stated Rupert was born with Down's Syndrome. Alice was by then forty-seven years old and George was fifty-nine. Rupert was a happy child and everyone loved him.

Alice fulfilled well her role as mistress of Eriboll and saw to it that all was done to establish the position of the family. A Clarke family crest was registered. This was based on the Clan Mackay crest, which consists of a hand holding a dagger with the motto 'Manu Forte'. The Clarke crest had the addition of a thistle behind the hand and then initials 'G.G.C.' below. This crest was then inscribed on the Clarke cutlery and was also cut into a seal for imprinting the sealing wax on legal documents.

Eriboll gave a welcome to many travellers. In the course of a speech, which he made at the coming of age of Allan Gilmour, Rosehall in 1910, Andrew Carnegie related how he had travelled through the north with Dr Hew Morrison and had come to Eriboll where, 'the late Mr Clarke of Eriboll' invited them to stay for lunch. Andrew Carnegie explained to George Granville how he was looking to buy a place in the Highlands to which George Granville replied that there was a property in Sutherland for sale, 'and, if he had the money it would not be long for sale,

48 From letters which Alice Gibson sent home from Russia to her family in England. These have been typed out by my daughter, Jane F. Clarke.

KEMPY HOUSE AND BAY LOCH ERIBOL

Kempie House and the boundary dyke of Heilim Hirsel, c. 1900.

because he would own it himself'. The place was Skibo and the rest is history.[49]

And Hugh Miller, the famous son of Cromarty, stonemason, geologist and editor of the *The Witness* newspaper, was also entertained at Eriboll. There is a signed copy of his book, *My Schools and Schoolmasters*, in the possession of my family, given by the author to George Granville with thanks for hospitality received.

Alice saw to it that Reay's education was that of a successful flockmaster's son. He was first sent to Alton Burn, a boarding preparatory school in Nairn. This was followed by four years at Trinity College, Glenalmond, the public school in Perthshire where he excelled in shooting and was a member of the Bisley VIII. He was then sent for a year as a farm pupil at Rothiebrisbane in Aberdeenshire with James Durno, his future father-in-law, a farm and farmer noted for the breeding of pedigree Shorthorn cattle and Clydesdale horses. His education was

49 *Highland News*, 3 September 1910. Also the *Northern Times* on 22 November 2003 in a letter from Dr Malcolm Bangor-Jones. I would record my grateful thanks to Dr Malcolm Bangor-Jones both for this letter and for the next three press reports on events at Eriboll.

completed by a year at the College of Agriculture in Aberdeen. He then returned to help with the management of Eriboll. In 1914 he also took on the tenancy of Edderton Farm in Easter Ross. Reay did not serve in the armed forces during the 1914–1918 war as he qualified for exemption from military service, being in a reserved occupation.

There were problems, as there are in any family. Understandably perhaps, there was discord between Alice and some of the children of George's first marriage. Jack in particular, the third child, did not get on at all well with his stepmother. Around 1898 when he was in his mid-thirties, he was sent down to Tain to sell the annual draft of cattle from Eriboll as his father was unwell and unable to go. The cattle sold well. Jack then set himself up on the proceeds at the Royal Hotel for the next week. When he did arrive back at Eriboll, there was a serious row. As a result Jack left home, joined the Lovat Scouts and went off to the Boer War. At the end of that war he settled down to farm in Africa. He married a Boer lady and seems to have lived happily ever afterwards. In some legal papers of 1924 we have an address for Jack as: 'John Charles Clarke, Farmer, River Bank Farm, near Buluwayo, Rhodesia'. Kate Erskine (Alice's cousin) in a rather telling letter of 4 December 1943 to my mother, states:

Jack, the younger son, would have loved to continue farming in the north either at Eriboll or at Meddat but could not hit it off with Aunt Alice, so he joined the Lovat Scouts & went to the S African war & remained out there farming until he died about three years ago [1940]. Yr Reay is so like him. We all loved Jack, so good looking and so full of go, but he wanted work & a house of his own. He wanted to marry a Miss Harvey, whose people lived at Rosemount after my grandmother died, but he had no settled income and so could not marry, poor Jack.

In 1904 George Granville died in an Edinburgh nursing home. He died from a stomach ulcer and this may have been troubling him for some time. He was buried at Balnakiel in July of that year and it must been a very large funeral. Alice was left a widow and chose to live on at Eriboll and to run the farm. The leases of the Easter Ross farms, Meddat and Rosemount, seem to have come to an end or were surrendered. The assets of George's estate, mainly the stock and tenancy of Eriboll, were left in trust to the three children by his first marriage and to the two sons by his third marriage. His widow was to have the life rent of the estate. The executors were his widow, Alice, his second son, Jack, who was now farming in South Africa and Charles Mackenzie, British Linen Bank agent in Tain. The executors were responsible for the running of Eriboll and Alice and Charles Mackenzie ran it. They had a really excellent head shepherd and manager in Donald Mackay as well as fine, experienced shepherds. However there cannot have been any contribution from Jack Clarke in faraway South Africa and not a lot from Charles Mackenzie in distant Tain. Alice lived on at Eriboll and was nominally in charge of the farm but it would have been Donald Mackay, the farm manager and head shepherd, who carried the full responsibility. He would certainly have seen to it that all was done in proper order and in due season. Eriboll continued to be very well run. The Eriboll wether lambs at the Lairg sale always appeared among the top ten for farms in Sutherland.

Alice was clearly an able organiser. The *Northern Chronicle*, 4 November 1908, reported that the schoolchildren of Laid and Eriboll celebrated together the anniversary of the battle of Balaclava on Saturday, 24 October. It states that:

Mrs Clarke, Eriboll House, graciously entertained with her usual generosity and good taste the young guests, and much praise is due to her for the excellent manner in which the arrangements were carried through. She welcomed the young company, and paid Mr Sutherland [the schoolmaster at Laid] high tribute for his kindness and benevolence, and in his efforts to instill patriotic feelings into the young minds of our country . . . After partaking of a sumptuous dinner, the children engaged in games and sports, and prizes were awarded to successful competitors. Thereafter tea and sweets were served and with the usual loyal and patriotic toasts, the singing of 'Auld Lang Syne' and 'God save the King', the proceedings came to a happy termination.[50]

Three months later the *Northern Times* of 14 January 1909 reported that:

The New Year was ushered in here with the usual festivities and rejoicings . . . This year like other years, the rifle shooting, both for the short and long ranges, was the event of the day and was eagerly contested, especially as a medal and money prizes were awarded to the best shot. Mr Reay Clarke obtained the highest score.

Mrs Clarke, Eriboll House, graciously patronised the proceedings by her presence and awarded prizes to the successful competitors. In the evening a dance was held, and the rooms presented an unusually gay and animated appearance by the large turnout of braw lads and bonnie lassies. Mr Reay Clarke opened the dance, which was entered upon with the greatest zest and enjoyment.[51]

And again the *Inverness Courier* of 21 June 1911 reported that:

Eriboll was en fete on Wednesday last when Mr Reay F. Clarke attained his majority. The weather was magnificent

50 *Northern Chronicle*, 4 November 1908.
51 *Northern Times*, 7 November 1907. (Reprinted in *Northern Times*' Millenium Supplement of 28 December 2000.)

and the grounds looked their best. The children of the village arrived at 3 p.m. and tea, sports and a scramble for sweets occupied the time till 6 p.m., when the dinner guests began to arrive. The guests were so numerous that the long tables in the dining room had to accommodate them in relays.

Indeed there is a large silver cup in the possession of our family. It is inscribed: 'Presented to Reay F. Clarke on attaining his Majority by friends at Eriboll and Tain.'[52]

There is also a letter, dated 28 February 1919, to R. F. Clarke Esqr., which reads:

Sir

Enclosed please find as per list £5 :15: 6. as a token of goodwill from the Eriboll people on the occasion of your marriage. As we cannot think what you would like, we thought it best to send you the money and you and the future Mrs Clarke can buy something suitable to remind you of the Eriboll people. With heartiest congratulations and every good wish for your future welfare and happiness from all.

Yours Respectfully,
Donald Mackay. (Head Shepherd)

Times were changing. Early in the Great War a Minister of the British government had travelled to Inverness and, in a recruiting speech, had promised that the land which had been taken from the people of the Highlands would be returned to them as soon as the war was won. James Hunter, in an article in the *Scotsman* of 26 August 1983, writes: 'While on a recruiting drive in Inverness at the height of the first World War a Government Minister

52 *Northern Chronicle,* 21 June 1911.

had declared: "The land question in the Highlands must be settled once and for all. Everyone is agreed that the people of the Highlands must be placed in possession of the soil." The young men of the north did rally to the Colours and they did so in quite extraordinary numbers. The multitude of the names of the fallen engraved on War Memorials in every town and village in the Highlands bears witness to the resounding response to that call and to that promise.'

In 1917 there arose the shameful affair of the Eilean Choraidh (O.S. spelling) or Choarie Island; there are various spellings. Choarie Island extends to about eighty acres. It lies towards the south end of Loch Eriboll and is about six hundred yards from the shore below Laid and twice that, some 1,200 yards, from the shore on the Eriboll side of the loch. It is thus much nearer to Laid than it is to Eriboll. It is a fine, green fertile island of limestone. On it Lord Reay had built a kiln for burning the lime and a pier for exporting the burnt lime. In former times there had been a thriving community there who worked the land.

A record which we have of this is the *Baptismal Roll for the Parish of Durness*. For the eight years between 1770 and 1778, there are entries of at least twelve baptisms for children born on Choarie Island. In the 'Prefatory Note' the editor, Dr Hew Morrison, states with regard to the Rev. John Thomson, the minister for the parish of Durness: 'He could not master the spelling of the local popular surnames, but he has preserved in the register a careful and minute phonetic rendering both of the names of persons and places.' The entries are interesting. For example:

7th August 1775   Hugh Macuillam Machustain, alias Morrison, in Island-a-Choarie, alias Islandhall. Ann.

25th March 1776   Wm. Macnish mac Dholicustian alias Mackay, tailor and tenent in Island Choarie. Angus.

13th June 1776   Hugh Mackay, alias Macen mhic En
mhic Dholicuilleam, tenent in Island
Choarie, lately in Shinnins. John.[53]

There was a strong community on Choarie Island in those days.
These small tenants were cleared and Choarie Island then
became a part – and a most valuable part – of the sheep farm of
Eriboll. The tups were put over there after they were clipped in
June. They would have done well and probably remained there
until tupping time in November. There is an old bothy on the
island in which the shepherd, who herded them, stayed.

It does appear that there was a very strong feeling – with
good reason – among the crofting community at Laid that Eilean
Choraidh should be leased to them and not be a part of Eriboll
farm. The 1898 Report of the Crofters' Commission records that
in March 1897 the Commissioners had considered an application from five Laid crofters that Corrie (sic) Island and part of
Polla hirsel should be assigned to them. The proprietor (Duke
of Sutherland) and the Eriboll farm tenant objected on the basis
that only five crofters of the Laid township had made this application. Were all the crofters in Laid to apply, then proprietor
and tenant would agree that the whole of Laid hirsel should be
assigned. There is no word of Choraidh Island. It seems that the
whole of Polla hirsel was being offered instead of the island. At
first the crofters accepted this and it was agreed by all that the
lands (Polla Hirsel only) to be assigned were the lands offered by
the proprietor and would be accepted by the crofters. However it
was then recorded that the applicants (the crofters), 'have taken
the extreme course of repudiating the Minute lodged by them,
and refusing to accept the decision of the Commissioners giving
effect thereto, it is not without considerable difficulty that the
Commissioners have allowed the withdrawal proposed'. It does

---

53 Dr Hew Morrison, Editor, *The Baptismal Roll of the Parish of Durness* c.
1890.

look as though it was the island that the crofters really wanted. The offer of the whole of Polla hirsel was just not good enough. From the tenant's (Clarke's) point of view it was much better to lose Polla hirsel than the island. Polla was an eild herding and the times when it was profitable to keep wethers had gone but the island was most valuable grazing for the farm's tups. This was the first incident – and there would be many more in the future – when the needs of the crofters were misunderstood or misinterpreted by government organisations.

In 1916 German submarine attacks on British shipping were causing a serious shortage of food in the country. Executive Food Production Committees were set up in each county and a call went out for all on the land to increase food production. In answer to this call, the crofters at Laid applied for permission to go over to Choarie Island and grow a crop of oats there. This was granted under the Defence of the Realm Regulations and fifteen Laid crofters were given possession of half an acre each on Choarie Island after they had given 'guarantees of cultivation and peaceful evacuation when required to do so'.

Accordingly, on Monday, 23 April 1917, a boatload of Laidonians plus the Reverend Adam Gunn, the Durness Parish minister, crossed the loch. The first sod was turned, the old well was cleared and the seven and a half acres were measured off, on and beside the Roan Mhor (the big field). This was the best field on the island. It had once yielded eighty bolls of oatmeal, milled by the miller at Bodi-havish. A boll weighs 140 lbs, which means that the field must have yielded almost five tons of oatmeal (80 x 140 =11,200 lbs) in that year. The party returned to Laid well pleased with the day's work.

Soon after, fifteen men of Laid returned, dug the seven and a half acres with the spade, harrowed the ground and sowed the oats. Many of these were fathers of the seventeen young men who were then with the army fighting in France and of whom five had already been killed. The oats grew well. The Board of Agriculture

had agreed to supply and erect a fence across the island to protect the oats from the Eriboll tups. However the Board was late
in getting this fence erected and, before it was, the Eriboll tups
were sent over to the island and, of course, ate the growing oats.
The *Northern Times* of 14 February 1918 states that Mr Andrew
Lindsay, convener of Sutherland County Council and a member of
the Food Production Committee: '. . . when he visited the island
in June last, he found the corn was eaten as bare as the floor of
the office by tups belonging to the late Mr Clarke's trustees' and
'Notwithstanding the damage done to the crops by the tups, the
corn grew to a height of four feet six inches. The straw was good,
but the grain was not up to much.'

And there was more. The grass grew well between the plots of
oats but, when the crofters asked if they might cut it and make
it into hay, Mr Charles Mackenzie, the British Linen Bank agent
in Tain and one of the late G. G. Clarke's trustees, threatened to
interdict them for removing the grass.[54] Naturally the committee was furious and unanimously agreed to apply for powers to
take over the whole island, which application was never granted.
The conduct of the Clarke Trustees was disgraceful and has gone
down in history as being disgraceful. The whole episode was only
a foretaste of how, within the next decade, further firm promises
made to the crofters by the British government were going to be
broken.

Laid, that exposed strip of peat hags, acid soil and rocks, which
lies along the western shore of Loch Eriboll, was a poor site for
establishing a crofting community. Yet it was there that those
whom Lord Reay had cleared from the lands of Eriboll on the
fertile eastern shore of Loch Eriboll and elsewhere were allowed
to settle. There is the tale of a ceilidh held in Laid during the closing days of the Second World War. The conversation turned to

54 *Northern Times*, 26 April 1917; *Highland News*, 4 August 1917; *Northern
Times*, 14 February 1918. My thanks are due to Dr Malcolm Bangor-Jones
for obtaining these press cuttings for me.

the pressing problem of what should be done with Adolf Hitler, were he to fall alive into the hands of the advancing allies. 'He should be hanged,' someone said. There was no dissent but some thought hanging was not sufficient punishment for one whose crimes were so monstrous. 'Perhaps he should be tortured first,' it was suggested. 'No! No! No!' said an old woman, who had so far not taken any part in the discussion, 'he deserves much worse than that. He should be given a croft in Laid.'[55]

The Board of Agriculture had been given authority to establish smallholdings under various Acts of Parliament and had set to after the war to purchase sheep farms for this purpose, particularly in the north of Scotland. Durness had been a parish with a history of disturbances on the issue of the lack of smallholdings and it was natural for the Board to direct their attention to that parish. The sheep farms of Balnakiel, Keoldale and Eriboll were all studied as to their suitability for being divided up into smallholdings. Early on Balnakiel was dropped. In 1919 Keoldale was purchased by the Board from the trustees of the late John C. Robertson, Fodderty, who had recently died. He had purchased it just the previous year from Mr W. E. Gilmour of Rosehall. Also in 1919, Eriboll was bought by the Board from Mr W. E. Gilmour for £12,000. The Board then had to obtain vacant possession of these farms, which they now owned, by giving the tenants notice to quit and by arranging for valuations of the sheep stocks. The Board would then divide the farms up into smallholdings or sheep stock clubs – or both – for the returned ex-servicemen and try to get the new smallholders to take over the sheep stocks. It was quite a task. The normal procedure at such a valuation was for the outgoing tenant to appoint his valuer and the incoming tenant to appoint his valuer. These two valuers would then meet and agree on the appointment of an oversman – a man of skill. It was the oversman who, having heard the opinions in detail of

55 It was the late Anson Mackay who told me this tale.

the two valuers as to the merits and demerits of the ewes and lambs, of the eild stock and of the tups, then determined the actual and final value of the stock. However at Keoldale and at Eriboll this practice was not followed. At both farms both parties – the outgoing tenants and the incoming Board of Agriculture – agreed that John R. Campbell of Shinness should act as the sole valuer. His valuation would be final and binding. He was duly appointed and accepted appointment – in the case of Eriboll by a deed dated 21 May 1921, just a few days before the actual valuation. This was signed in Edinburgh by the chairman and secretary of the Board of Agriculture and at Eriboll by Alice Gibson Clarke for the trustees of the late G. G. Clarke. The witnesses to her signature were Ian M. Campbell, J. R. Campbell's son, and Donald Mackay, Sheep Manager at Eriboll.[56] It was an unusual decision.

John R. Campbell was most highly regarded throughout the Highlands as a noted flockmaster, judge and valuer. He was faced with a difficult task at Eriboll as the sole valuer. He must have had considerable sympathy for Alice Gibson, the widow of his old friend, the late George Granville Clarke. She was being turned out of her farm and her home. Eriboll, that renowned sheep farm, was to be handed over to crofters. Sheep prices were then enjoying a post-war boom and were at a peak. The cheque for the sheep stock would be coming, not from a fellow sheep farmer, but from the Government.

However there is no doubt that John Campbell carried out a thoroughly professional and skilled valuation of the sheep stocks both at Keoldale and at Eriboll. Keoldale had a greater number of sheep. He valued these at a lower figure than the Eriboll stock. His valuation at Keoldale was later reluctantly accepted by the Durness ex-servicemen although there were problems. Keoldale was formed

56 A copy of this deed was given to me by Mrs Sue Campbell, Balblair, widow of the late Colin Campbell, who was a grandson of John R. Campbell of Shinness.

into a sheep stock club and today it still runs successfully. John Campbell considered the Eriboll stock, especially the ewes and lambs, a better stock than Keoldale and valued them at a higher figure. The Eriboll ewes and lambs were valued at £10: 5/- each. This valuation was to have serious consequences in the years that lay ahead, which I shall describe in the next chapter. At the end of May 1921, John Campbell issued his award. The executors of the late George Granville Clarke received a cheque for £43,023:13: 7 and Alice Gibson left Eriboll. It was the end of an era.

The years that followed did not bring Alice Gibson much happiness. She had been taking money out of the late George Granville Clarke's Trust without authority. She had spent this largely on consultant's fees, medical care and other expenses for her son, Rupert. The family of George Granville's first wife sued her and her fellow trustee, Charles Mackenzie, for breach of trust. The case was first heard in the Sheriff Court in Tain where she lost. She appealed, it was heard in the High Court in Edinburgh and she lost again. By this time she was almost eighty years old.

After just sixteen years of marriage, Alice Gibson had been left a widow in 1904. Then the final eight years of her life were filled with misfortune. In 1920 her beloved son, Rupert, had died at the age of twenty-eight. In 1921 she had to leave Eriboll, which she loved and which had been her home for the past thirty-three years. And, in 1925, she had to try to defend her actions in court and had failed.

She lived out her life in a succession of houses in Easter Ross, ending up at 'The Whins', Nigg. There she went down to the beach in Nigg Bay each morning and drank a pint of sea water. In a photograph taken of her at that time she is a tall, upright figure. There is no hint of the trials that had afflicted her.

She wrote the following poem for her neighbour, Mrs Douglas, Nigg Mains:

Ode.
To the Chatelaine of Nigg House by Alice Gibson
Clarke. Jan 5th 1925.

> A lady 'Douglas' was her name
> Possessed a garden of much fame,
> Thence flowers she often culled for me
> Blossoms delighting heart and ee!
> Roses, sweet peas and mignonette,
> From palest pink to darkest jet.
> How can I this good friend repay
> For all she doeth day by day?
> Return I cannot make tis clear
> Save knowledge, that to me, she's dear.

Alice Gibson died at 'The Whins', Nigg, in 1928. She was eighty-two years old. She is buried in Tain, refusing to be buried in the family plot at the Balnakiel cemetery. Space had been left for her name on the tombstone there, which marks the spot where George Granville's first two wives are interred. Alice 'was not going in beside those other two women'.

11

The Valuation at Eriboll and Its Consequences

In his book *Highland Memories* Colin Macdonald writes:

A sheep stock valuation day was a day to be enjoyed and remembered. To it would gather farmers from all over the county, and some from beyond. The neighbouring ones brought their shepherds to give a hand to ensure that every sheep in its class was properly shown to the valuators. Usually there were two of these – one representing the interests of the outgoing tenant and the other the incoming. There was an oversman in case of non-agreement; and, as each valuator was all out for his own side, non-agreement was frequent and the oversman was the person who really mattered. This highly important person was 'mutually chosen' by the parties to the valuation. Not infrequently it took many months of mutual and highly diverting sparring for position before the choice could be announced. When no agreement could be arrived at, the appointment of the oversman was remitted to the Sheriff of the county. But the knowledge that in the end they would almost certainly have to submit to the oversman in no wise dampened the valuators' ardour in promoting the interests of their respective clients, and their ingenuity and resource in that direction was always a thing to marvel at. In a case where the incoming tenant's expert gives it as his emphatic opinion 'before God and with a good conscience' that the gimmers would be dear at £4 apiece, and the expert for the outgoing, under similar solemn guidance and restraint, is equally emphatic that they would be cheap at £6, there is obviously consider-able scope for persuasive argument. Variety in technique was infinite. There might be audibly expressed horror at the other's awful position *vis-à-vis* his Creator; or it might be a whispered (but just audible) concern that neighbours should never be allowed to know the sort of fool he is making of himself in suggesting such an absurd price.[57]

Eriboll was a bound stock, which meant that the sheep stock was bound to the land and could not be dispersed or sold. At a waygoing the incoming tenant, in this case the Board of Agriculture, had to take over the entire sheep stock at whatever figure might be fixed by valuation. Such a valuation was a skilled task. A bound sheep stock represented a capital asset with a value well beyond the price those sheep would make if they were sold in the open market. Accordingly they had to be valued and not only did the valuer have to decide on a fair value for each sheep according to its character, quality and condition but he also had two additions to make. He was required to add a figure for hefting and a figure for acclimatisation.

Hefting was added because the ingrained hefting instinct of a bound sheep stock ensured that those sheep would stay on their heft and not wander off across the unfenced hills of Sutherland. Certainly the odd one might stray but a good shepherd would know that they had strayed, probably know where they had gone, find them and bring them back and hold them on their heft. If a hefted ewe was moved off her hirsel for a handling or because of a snowstorm, then that ewe would make her way back to her own heft just as soon as ever she was able to do so. To build this asset of hefting into a sheep stock took years of careful herding and was clearly a part of the capital value of that stock.

Acclimatisation was added because, over the generations, the sheep of that farm had acquired a certain ability to withstand the

57 Colin Macdonald, *Highland Memories*, 1949.

particular diseases which might afflict the stock on that particular hirsel. It was a matter of survival of the fittest. Those prone to disease would die. It was from the ones which did not die that the future generations were bred. Also shepherds were greatly skilled in knowing their hirsels and in knowing those parts where the sheep must not be allowed to graze at certain times of the year if losses – for example from diseases such as trembling – were to be kept under some kind of control. Today this problem of disease is dealt with largely by inoculation with preventative vaccines and by adding mineral supplements to their diet. However, in the times of which we write, carbon tetrachloride capsules for the prevention of liver fluke were about the only remedy in the war against disease and even they were only just starting to be introduced.

To determine the value of the Eriboll sheep stock, as mentioned in the previous chapter, John R. Campbell of Shiness was appointed sole valuer. He was mutually appointed both by the incoming tenant, the Board of Agriculture, and by the outgoing tenant, the executors of the late George Granville Clarke. It was not a normal arrangement. The Board of Agriculture had bought Eriboll at Martinmas 1919 from W. E. Gilmour for £12,000. A year and a half later, on 21 May 1921, the deed appointing John R. Campbell as sole arbiter was signed at Eriboll. It is odd that it took eighteen months for the deed authorising the appointment of a sole valuer to be agreed, drawn up and signed. It is possible that the delays in the normal appointment of an oversman by the two valuers, one acting for the outgoing tenant and one acting for the incoming tenant – as so graphically described by Colin Macdonald in the opening paragraph of this chapter – gave the Board much cause for concern. They were under serious pressure from the Durness ex-servicemen and others to get smallholdings established while the rules and regulations of the civil service were probably causing delays at every turn. However, in the end, John R. Campbell was appointed sole valuer for the sheep stocks and the farm stock both at Keoldale and at Eriboll and the valuations could go ahead. The actual arrangements on these farms for all the work of gathering the sheep, sorting and holding them and then returning them to their hirsels must have been already discussed, planned and agreed.

The Eriboll valuation was described to me by Ian M. Campbell, John R. Campbell's son, who kept The Book for his father. The Book was of critical importance. In The Book the numbers of each class of sheep and their value, as declared by John Campbell, were most carefully recorded. The count would be done probably by the head shepherd and checked by Ian Campbell. Keoldale was valued one day and that night the Campbells stayed at Eriboll. The next day Eriboll was valued.

'The Account of the Valuations of the Sheep Stock, & etc. at Eriboll, Sutherlandshire, taken over by the Board of Agriculture for Scotland from the Trustees of the late George Granville Clarke, at Whitsunday 1921' reads:

2,333 ewes with lambs	@ £10: 5/- each less 1 shott per 20 at 1/3 less
10 grit ewes	@ £9 each
264 eild ewes	@ £7 each less 1.5 shotts per 20 @ 1/3 less
672 gimmers	@ £7 each less ½ shott per 20 @ 1/3 less
826 ewe hoggs	@ £6:15/- each less ½ shotts per 20 @ 1/3 less
450 2 yr old wethers	@ 90/- each less 1.5 shotts per 20 @ 1/3 less
446 1 yr old wethers	@ 80/- each less 2 shotts per 20 @ 1/3 less

117 tups valued individually to average £19 each

5,118 sheep plus the lambs.   Total value £41,483: 5/-

Cattle, horses, crop, cultivations etc.

Total value <u>£1,488:14: 6</u>

TOTAL: <u>£42,971:19: 6</u>

<u>Expenses:</u> Submission	£4: 4: 2
Valuator's fee	£50: 0: 0

Hire of cars for transport of valuator and shepherds

<u>£49: 4: 0</u>

TOTAL: <u>£103: 8: 2</u>

Half to be paid by outgoing – the Clarkes

£51:14: 1

Half to be paid by incoming – the Board of Agriculture

£51:14: 1

Total proceeds from valuation	£42,971:19: 6
Expenses which have been added	<u>£51:14: 1</u>
The Clarkes received a cheque for:	<u>£43,023:13: 7</u>

There is an error in this account. The expenses amounted to £103: 8: 2. Half – £51:14:1 – should have been charged to the Board of Agriculture and half – the same sum, £51:14:1 – deducted from the Clarke's cheque. However instead of deducing this from the Clarke's cheque, this sum has been added to their final payment. The Clarkes therefore received a cheque for £43,023:13: 7 when they should have received £42,920: 5: 5. The Clarkes got £103: 8: 2 too much!

The arithmetic to work out the total value for the sheep stock as £41,483: 5/- was difficult. Again, in his book *Highland Memories*, Colin Macdonald states, when writing of calculating the value of sheep stock:

Even with the help of their legal agents the best that could be obtained sometimes was agreement to split the difference between their respective totals that represented hours of laborious calculations. It was the late William Maclennan, for many years factor for Lord Zetland, who about forty years ago first made such calculations easy by the tables in his ready reckoner, *The Flockmaster's Companion* ". . . all you had to do was to multiply the total number of sheep in each class by the appropriate figure" (as given in the ready reckoner tables).

Colin Macdonald continues,

William did not visualise any figure above £70 per clad score for ewes and lambs. In 1920–21 and again recently ewes and lambs were going at over £200 per clad score and we had to juggle with the tables.

Colin Macdonald was writing in 1949 and I wonder if his thoughts were going back to the Keoldale and Eriboll valuations of 1921 and the consequences thereof.[58]

There is an interesting item of expenditure in this statement of the Eriboll valuation which reads: 'Cost of cars in connection with Valuator and taking Shepherds and assistant Shepherds to the different hirsels quickly to mark sheep and lambs so as to mother the lambs properly . . . £49: 4/-.'

What would that hire of £49: 4/- cost today? How many cars were there? Where did the cars come from? Where all did they take the shepherds? How many shepherds? And what about the dogs?

It was an enormous undertaking and must have taken skilled planning with great understanding of the needs of the sheep. These 5,118 sheep plus the lambs had been gathered off the 30,000 acres of Eriboll and sorted. The ewe hoggs and the gimmers

58 Colin Macdonald, *Highland Memories*, 1949.

would have been running with the ewes and so would have had to be shed off. The different lots would then have been run past John Campbell for him to make his valuation. A valuation mark would have been buisted on every sheep so that any unmarked stragglers, which came in with later gatherings, could be added to the count. What then? Were the lambs shed off to be cut and marked or was this left for another gathering? If they were marked, it must have added greatly to the problem of getting 2,333 lambs correctly mothered up with 2,333 ewes and then driven back to their hirsels.

There were only two fanks at Eriboll which are accessible by road; one at Cashel Dhu, said to be the largest fank in north Sutherland, and one at Faoilinn. There would also have been pens at the Eriboll steading. Some of the sheep may have been held overnight in the parks at Eriboll. By any standards it was an outstanding feat to get 5,118 sheep plus the lambs gathered, sorted, checked, counted and then run slowly past the valuer on that day at the end of May 1921. We could not do it today. Then all the sheep had to be herded back to their hirsels. How many shepherds were involved? And how many shepherds from neighbouring farms? And how many wives took on the task of feeding them all? They would all have had to be fed. There is no mention in the 'Account of the Valuation' of any payments to extra shepherds nor to the wives, yet all the shepherds from nearby would have come in to help and many others as well.

John R. Campbell was seventy-two years old when he valued the Keoldale and Eriboll sheep stocks. Ian Campbell, his son, was then twenty-five years old. Fifty years later he told me how the two of them had stayed on that night at Eriboll. His father was tired with the two days of valuation – Keoldale the first day and Eriboll the following day – and he did not come down the next morning. About ten o'clock he sent for Ian and told him to read through The Book, while he remained in bed. He said that Ian was to stop if he raised his hand as he might want to change an item. Ian then read slowly through The Book, the whole of the valuations both at Keoldale and at Eriboll. It took him well over an hour. His father listened most carefully but never once raised his hand. When all had been read, John just said that he was satisfied and he would sign The Book as it was a correct valuation. The cattle, horses, implements and other items were valued later that day and all was sent to Mactavish and Mackenzie, the instructing solicitors in Tain.

On the evening of that May term when the valuation of the sheep stock and the other tenant's stock and crop had been completed, the Board of Agriculture became responsible for the running of Eriboll. It seems that the shepherds and other staff stayed on apart from Donald Mackay, the manager and head shepherd. It is likely that he retired and moved away. It is said that it was the aforementioned Colin Macdonald, now an inspector with the Board of Agriculture, who became responsible for running Eriboll. Colin Macdonald had been born and brought up on a croft on the Heights of Inchvannie, Strathpeffer and had been specially selected to go to the College of Agriculture in Aberdeen where he successfully obtained a diploma. He was then appointed agricultural adviser in the Western Isles before being transferred to the Board of Agriculture. Colin Macdonald was destined for a remarkable career in the agricultural departments of the government before being appointed the Gaelic-speaking member of the Scottish Land Court. His books are a most valuable and almost unique record of life in the crofting communities in the first half of the twentieth century. However the coming of a civil servant to take charge of Eriboll cannot have been popular amongst a conservative bunch of shepherds. They heartily disliked any change. Colin Macdonald's presence at Eriboll was resented and his job would have been made as difficult as possible. Years later I can remember asking a shepherd who had been in that district during those years, if he had known Colin Macdonald. His reply was to the effect that Colin Macdonald was only a crofter's son from the Heights of Achterneed and what in the world would he know about sheep. The ill-feeling and resentment between crofter, the native, and shepherd, the incomer, was still very much alive although it was, by then, three generations since that shepherd's family had come north with the sheep from the Borders.

However Eriboll was now owned and occupied by the Board of Agriculture and had to be farmed to the best of the Board's ability while the mechanism of government set to work to divide it up into smallholdings and a sheep stock club. In 1922, the 5,500 acres of the Polla hirsel, which marched with Laid, were detached from Eriboll and let for an annual rent of £55 to fifteen Laid crofters as an extension to their grazings. It is not recorded what happened to the sheep stock there. It seems that the Laid crofters were not required to take them over as the issue of their worth does not appear to have arisen.

A letter to the *Northern Ensign*, dated 19 April 1922 and signed by 'Radical Mackay, Reay Country', sets out very clearly the local feeling about Eriboll at that time. He states:

On March 31st the Board of Agriculture came to Eriboll Farm . . . for the purpose of arranging with the smallholders for the allocation of holdings. Seventeen ex-servicemen turned out expecting they were to receive land on reasonable terms as a result of the Board's visit but they soon learned they were mistaken. When the terms were read out to the men they discovered that they were expected to pay £400 before they would get possession of a holding. How could ex-servicemen, who had served for four years in the trenches at 1s 3d per day and had then been unemployed for over a year, be expected to have the capital to purchase stock and build a house?

He goes on to explain that the arable land on Eriboll extended to ten parks of twenty acres each and a man would need to be given a croft of twenty acres before he could be expected to build a house on it. He continues: 'Is it not high time to bring the whole matter before the government who gave pledges to ex-servicemen? It would be well to find out if this is the way the men are to be dealt with who shed their blood for King and Country in the most cruel and inhuman warfare ever waged on the continent of Europe.' He goes on to deplore the appointment of a single valuer, the high value placed on the sheep stock and other matters. He closes: 'Let the ex-servicemen form themselves into an Association and demand from the Government, who gave the pledge, the fulfillment thereof.'[59]

The matter rolled on. The management of Eriboll must have been difficult. Shepherds dislike change and any farm staff dislikes uncertainty about the future. Prices were falling seriously and this would have affected the returns from the shepherds' packs. If Eriboll was to be broken up into smallholdings and a sheep stock club, there would be fewer jobs there in the future. It was not a good time for the wellbeing of Eriboll and its sheep stock. Nor can it have been a good time for the staff of the Board of Agriculture, especially Colin Macdonald, charged with creating these changes. On the one hand there was the bitterness and ill-feeling from the Durness ex-servicemen in that they had been promised land and they were not getting it. On the other hand the Treasury was critical of the conduct of the Board of Agriculture in that a very large sum of government money had been spent on getting Eriboll for the resettlement of ex-servicemen and no ex-servicemen had been resettled there.

Following the unsatisfactory meeting between the Board and the seventeen ex-servicemen at Eriboll on 31st March 1921, fourteen months later, at Whitsunday 1922, the Board issued

---

59 Radical Mackay, *Northern Ensign*, Wick, 19 April 1922. Once again I am deeply grateful to Dr Malcolm Bangor-Jones for obtaining for me, not just this letter, but all the press cuttings, letters and Hansard Reports that cover these events.

Eriboll Lodge c. *1923.*

a further invitation by advertisement and by notice in the local post office for applicants to come forward. No one applied. At Whitsunday 1923 invitations were again advertised and again no one applied. It was now two years since the Treasury had paid out that £43,023:13: 7 to the Clarkes and no progress at all had been made in achieving the object for which that money had been spent. The matter rolled on.

Two and half years later in December 1925, Mr E. St. J. Bamford, who may have been a minister in the government or a senior civil servant, wrote to the King's and Lord Treasurer's Remembrancer (K. & L.T.R.) – in a way the Treasury – 'it seems very desirable to get rid of this expensive incubus [Eriboll] and perhaps you will advise as to Mr Mather's question'. Five days later, on 16 December, Mr Adam of K. & L.T.R. was replying, 'It seems desirable to sell this estate in order to get rid of the heavy cost of management etc. as soon as possible . . .'

This is understandable. By July of the previous year (1925) the value of the sheep stock had fallen from £41,483 to £23,454.

This was a loss on the sheep stock of £18,029, although the disposal of the Polla hirsel should be allowed for. Under the Board's management the value of the Eriboll sheep stock had almost halved in four years.

Accordingly on 18 March 1926, Messrs Knight, Frank and Rutley, Estate Agents, Edinburgh were instructed to offer Eriboll for sale by auction with an upset price of £10,000, which was £2,000 below the price at which the Board had bought the farm in 1919. There were no bidders. During the coming months the agents twice more offered the farm by auction and again there were no bidders. Then it is said – and it is a splendid story – that Mr Jock Elliot, who was a leading flockmaster in the Borders, just turned up unannounced at St Andrew's House in Edinburgh asking to see his cousin, Walter Elliot, the Secretary for Scotland (the post did not become a Secretary of State until 1928). It seems that Jock Elliot, there and then and without ceremony, made a verbal offer for Eriboll. It was almost certainly very thankfully received although, of course, we do not know what was said. This discussion was followed by a written offer from Mr Elliot, which is contained in a letter dated 6 September 1926, whereby he offered to buy Eriboll for £10,000 plus the sheep stock, which was to be valued at Martinmas that year by a single valuer, Mr Frank Thomson. There is an internal letter of 9 September from the Board of Agriculture to the Secretary of the Treasury seeking confirmation of authority to accept this offer and ends, 'and the sooner the running loss on the estate [Eriboll] is brought to an end, the better'. The valuation, again with a single valuer as at Whitsunday 1921, must have followed at the term of Martinmas 1926.

The scene now moves to London, to the House of Commons. Some two weeks later, the storm started in the House of Commons. Sir Archibald Sinclair, Member of Parliament for Caithness and Sutherland, and the local M.P., led a very effective attack on the government's handling of the Eriboll affair. Sir John Gilmour was now the Secretary for Scotland and he had to do his best to defend the Board of Agriculture's actions. For the next six months that storm continued unabated. Six times did Sir Archibald, supported by others, raise the matter on the floor of the House of Commons with Sir John Gilmour trying again and again to defend the actions of his Board of Agriculture.

The figures spoke for themselves:

1919: The Board spent £12,000 buying the estate of
Eriboll   £12,000

1921: The Board spent £43,023 buying the stock on
Eriboll   £43,023

                                                           £55,023

1926: The Board received £10,000 for the estate of
Eriboll   £10,000

and £9,388 for the stock on Eriboll   £9,388

                                                           £19,388

                                            Loss   £35,635

The Board had lost £35,635 on the taking over of Eriboll. If a factor of fifty is used to bring these figures up to present day values, then the Board of Agriculture had lost around £1,500,000 on the Eriboll transactions. There were still neither smallholdings nor a sheep stock club there for the returned ex-servicemen of Durness.

On 9 May 1927 there was a full debate in the House of Commons on Eriboll and the actions of the Board of Agriculture. This started at 6 p.m. and finished over three hours later after 9 p.m. The arguments continued along the same lines with Sir Archibald Sinclair leading the attack as energetically as ever. Basically the question asked was why had the Clarkes been paid £43,023 for the sheep stock on Eriboll when the Board sold the same stock for £9,388 a few years later? The answer was complicated, technical and most unsatisfactory. Towards the end of the debate an M.P., Mr Kidd, suggested rather weakly that, 'One thing has come out of this debate and that is, that we have at last laid the ghost of Eriboll.' In the end the matter was rather passed over but, soon afterwards, the Board of Agriculture was wound up and a new government body, The Department of Agriculture for Scotland, was appointed in its place.

For the next fifty-seven years Eriboll was farmed very successfully by Jock Elliot. Eriboll continued to be regarded as one of the foremost sheep stocks in the county of Sutherland. Hugh Mackay was long head shepherd there. Many years ago he told me that he always aimed to put a thousand wether lambs into his top draw for the Lairg Lamb Sale in August each year. He usually achieved this and all without any hand-feeding of the ewes. Jock Elliot and after his death his family continued to farm Eriboll until 1983 when they instructed Messrs Strutt and Parker, Estate Agents, in Edinburgh to sell Eriboll. Offers of over £500,000 were invited. Eriboll was sold soon afterwards for £425,000 – 'for the price of a couple of dingy semis in the affluent south', as the new owner described it. Once again, it was the end of an era.

12

The Manner of the Husbandry

The word is husbandry: and husbandry is what farming is, always has been, and is still – even now. The original meaning of the word 'to husband' is to administer as a good steward; to manage with thrift and prudence; also to save . . . Our question should be, not, is farming efficient, but is it husbandry? If the husbandry is good, then, and only then, will it be efficient. Husbandry conveys the concept of careful management, so as to obtain the greatest good: conservation of resources: a sense of cherishing: thrift: above all an awareness of responsibility and continuity. These virtues defy economic evaluation. That does not make them unworthy of consideration.

H. R. Fell[60]

When the Blackface and Cheviot sheep were first brought north, during the period centred on 1800, the money lay in the wool clip and thus the herding of these flocks was first organised with emphasis on wool production. Let us take a look at these farms, the manner of the husbandry and how the sheep were herded.

Patrick Sellar, in his account of his farming in Strathnaver in 1831, writes:

The pasturage consists of a great variety of plants, singularly adapted to the maintenance, during every month of the year, of the only domesticated animal [sheep] possessed of a cover adequate to defend it by day and night from the effects of such a climate . . . Where the waters, by cutting

60 H. R. Fell, *Proceedings of the Farmers' Club 1967.*

out ravines, glens, and straths, have formed an alluvial soil, composed of the debris of the mountain rocks mixed with peat, there the finer sorts of plants appear. These plants vary according to the quality of the component parts whereof the soil on which they grow consists. On spots, for instance, where the decomposing feldspar abounds, some natural clover, rye-grass, yarrow or mille-foil, mountain daisy, primrose, and other plants of first quality are discovered, – mixed with the holcus mollis, agrostes, airae, &c. which are natural to the decomposing mica, – with the fescue grasses, brome grass, common bent, heather, *et hoc genus omne*, which is content with the nourishment to be derived from the sterile bank of quartz gravel. In this respect the pastures of the county of Sutherland possess an advantage over many tracts exhibiting a more flattering outline; and with the ever varying proportions and combinations of matter contained in its gneiss, there is throughout the country an infinite mixture of the plants best suited for the maintenance of 'keeping stock' during every season of the year; which grasses, by the irregular bursting out of rocks in a state of partial decomposition, and by the serpentine course of the burns and waters, are ultimately interwoven with the alpine plants which grow upon the peat-bog, and form the principal part of the maintenance of the stock.

Of these alpine plants, there exists a considerable number and variety. On the knolls, the heather (erica vulgaris) prevails. It fills with seed, ripening in all seasons of ordinary fertility, like a field of corn,* and forms a principal part of the food of stock, during the wet months of October, November, December and January. In exposed situations, the shepherds burn it, and the sheep eat the young shoots in August and September. In lower positions it is left to

---

* In 1816 it [the heather] filled very imperfectly, and the consequences to the flocks were deeply felt during the coming months.

come to greater length, so that the sheep may work down to it in times of snow, and in order to afford shelter in lambing time. Adjoining the heather, the sheep find, on the peat of damp and deeper quality, the ling (erica tetralix), cotton grass (eriophorum vaginatum), rasp grass (carex caespitose). The leaves of these plants they consume along with the heather, during the autumn and winter months. In February, the heather has lost its seed. It is succeeded by the pry (carex panica), the stool bent (juncus squarrosus) and by thick beds of the flowers of the cotton grass, which are found in the latter end of February, and beginning of March, pointing with great vigour to the cheerless sun of that wet and uncomfortable season. These plants continue in use, until the second or third week of April; and during all this time they furnish for *keeping* stock, food of the best quality and in the greatest abundance. From this date to the middle of May, a link in this country is wanting in the chain of alpine eatage. On well drained and moderately stocked ground, the finer qualities, which in this season begin to spring, supply the defect, but under different management, the 'hunger rot' and a train of consequent ills sometimes ensue. In the middle May, however, the deer hair (scirpus caespitosus) takes the place of the moss. It shoots through the ground like a thick braid of corn, and with the fine grasses, by this time in full vigour, provides stock most abundantly, until the month of August; when the ground is lightened by the departure of the annual cast or sale lot sheep; and the young heather and ling come again into play.[61]

Patrick Sellar makes no mention of the shielings, yet these must have been numerous. They had provided all the summer

---

61 Patrick Sellar, *Farm Reports III County of Sutherland*, Library of Useful Knowledge, 1831.

grazing for the cattle and other stock of the tacksmen and their subtenants. Nor does he mention the fine, clean pasture that there must have been there, when he first leased those 70,000 acres or so in Strathnaver. He certainly makes a strong case for stocking those acres with sheep and dividing them up into ten hirsels, each with its own shepherd. What he does not foretell is the deterioration that this manner of grazing husbandry will bring to that countryside. The variety of species which he lists, are most unlikely to be found in quantity in Strathnaver today and certainly not in the abundance that he and his shepherds took for granted.

The Grazings

The grazings on a hirsel consisted of a small amount of greens with a grassy sward and a very large amount of outrun – heather and poorer grasses. Eriboll was divided up into seven hirsels and the average size of a hirsel was some 5,000 acres. Of this perhaps as little as 5%, 250 acres, would be greens and the balance, some 4,750 acres, would be outrun. These figures are very rough averages and varied greatly from hirsel to hirsel. Further there were no hard boundaries between greens and outrun for they merged, the one with the other. However it was the greens which supplied by far the most valuable and nutritious grazing and this had to be rationed. This was done by limiting the time which the sheep would be allowed to spend grazing the greens, as is described more fully in the chapter on herding. In the morning the shepherd would turn his sheep down from the higher ground on to these greens and then move them off again at the same time every afternoon. The greens would thus be stocked at a rate of maybe four or five sheep to the acre for the six or seven hours that they would be allowed to graze there. They were then spread out over the rest of the hirsel – the 4750 acres of outrun – for the remainder of the day and for the night. This gave a measure of grazing control without which the greens would have been rapidly destroyed by what would have been continuous defoliation.

The management of those parts of the outrun where there was a good growth of heather was carried out by muirburn. Very occasionally, if the weather was just right, some heather might be burnt in the back-end but the great bulk of the heather burning was done in March or early April before the lambing. The aim was to burn the heather as soon as it grew higher than a man's ankle. Burning it then, when it was still vigorously growing, meant that on a good site fresh re-growth would be starting again by the back-end. Young green heather was a most attractive feed for the sheep. They eagerly sought it out and throve on it. Herding was needed to see that it was not overgrazed in its early stages. Some long heather would be left unburnt for the sheep to work in when there was snow on the ground but the main aim was to have the bulk of the heather kept at or just below ankle height. Vigorous heather, growing at that height, brought a rich flowering in August which would be followed by the seedheads and these greatly helped to feed the sheep for much of the winter. That was the intention but it was hard to achieve. The weather had to be just right, dry with enough wind but not too much. Sufficient hands had to be available to control the fire with fire brooms and then there were the gamekeepers. When sporting rents began to rise, factors insisted that gamekeepers be given more and more say on how the heather was to be burnt and they wanted it burnt in a mosaic of narrow strips to meet the needs of the grouse. The days of when a big fire was a good fire came to an end and many were the rows between the keepers and the shepherds.

Wether Hirsels

The higher, poorer ground was set off as wether hirsels. These would be of 3000 acres or more, sometimes much more, with a shepherd living on and in charge of that hirsel. He would have a cottage there, usually with a meadow to make hay, a couple of cows (or goats) and a pack of a number of wethers of his own, which were herded along with the master's flock. These hirsels were stocked with perhaps 500 or more wethers, made up of roughly 170 sheep of each age – one-year-olds, two-year-olds, three-year-olds and possibly some four-year-olds. They were big strong sheep, hardy and capable of breaking out of snowdrifts. When they reached the autumn of their third year they would usually be cast i.e. sold to a lowground farmer who would then fatten them on turnip for sale to the butcher. The carcases made large joints of mature, well-flavoured mutton.

Wethers produce a heavier fleece than ewes. They do not require such good grazings as ewes, are easier to herd and live better. Therefore, in the early days and until maybe the mid-1800s, it was to create large wether stocks that the husbandry was directed. In those days it was the wethers that were the money-earners on the hill farms of Sutherland.

Ewe Hirsels

These were on the better ground and would be upwards of 3000 acres. They would be in the charge of one shepherd and he would often have a boy to help him. Again the shepherd would have a house on that hirsel and a byre. Near to the house would be a meadow where he would cut and make hay for winter keep for his cows. He would also have the right to cut and harvest peats. Again, as part of his wage, he would have a pack of his own stock – two or more cows plus their followers and thirty or forty ewes plus their followers. These would 'follow the master's flock', i.e. would be herded in amongst the farm's sheep belonging to the hirsel and would not receive any special food or attention – at least that was the theory. They were the property of the shepherd and he would receive the payment from the sale of the wool, the surplus lambs and the cast ewes of his pack.

Changes to the Wether and Ewe Hirsels

As the decades passed, the economics of hill sheep farming changed and, perforce, the stocking of the hirsels changed too. By the 1860s onward Australian wool had started to flood in to supply the woollen industries of England. Later, with the installation of refrigeration in ships, frozen lamb from New Zealand came too. This meant that there was less and less demand for home-produced wool and the housewife bought the small gigots of New Zealand lamb instead of the large joints of mature wether mutton. At the same time demand was starting to grow for grouse-shooting and deerstalking. A prospective tenant of a sporting estate would offer a much larger rent for higher ground than a hill farmer who was planning to rear wether sheep there. Many of the higher and more remote hirsels were cleared of sheep and turned into deer forests. The need then in hill farming was for more and more ewes because the money was now in the lamb crop and in the cast ewes – not in the wool. Previously the wool cheque had paid the rent and the shepherds' wages. Later the wool cheque would only pay the shepherds' wages. Today the wool cheque won't even do that.

All this brought great changes to the hill sheep farms and especially to the ewe hirsels. It was now important to stock the whole farm with the greatest numbers of ewes that it would possibly carry. Thus ewes were stocked on any and every hirsel that was at all capable of carrying them. Further the ewe hoggs were not returned to the ewe hirsel, where they had been born and reared, but, when they came back from wintering, they were moved out to one of the former wether hirsels. Some of these remained as part of that sheep farm and were not yet turned over to sport. There, these returned ewe hoggs joined the gimmers – and the few wethers still carried – to form an eild or non-breeding hirsel. They were a right problem for the shepherds as these hoggs were difficult to settle on this strange ground. They needed weeks of herding to get them to stay and not rush back towards where they had been reared. However the moving of the hoggs and maiden ewes out to these eild hirsels did allow greater numbers of ewes to be carried on the ewe hirsels. There was a further problem. When the maiden ewes were moved in the autumn from the eild hirsel back to the ewe hirsel, where they had been born, they now looked on that eild hirsel as home. It took almost as much herding to get them to settle on the ewe hirsel as it had taken to get them settled on the eild herding when they had returned as hoggs from the wintering eighteen months earlier. These changes were not popular with the shepherds. They vigorously maintained – and those that are left alive still do – that the sheep did not thrive nearly so well under this system of using eild hirsels to hold the ewe hoggs and gimmers for that year and a half as they did when the female stock spent their life – apart from one wintering – on the hirsel of their birth.

Regular Ages

On a ewe hirsel with a stock of four hundred ewes, each autumn the count would be:

- 180 ewe lambs if there had been a 90% lambing – away at wintering
- 170 wether lambs if there had been a 90% lambing – away at wintering
- 10 tup lambs if there had been a 90% lambing – away at wintering
- [These were the best male lambs, selected as future sires for the flock and left entire.]
- 100 gimmers 1.5 years old: not to be put to the tup that autumn

100 maiden ewes 2.5 years old: to be put to the tup that autumn

100 one-crop ewes 3.5 years old: to be put to the tup that autumn

100 two-crop ewes 4.5 years old: to be put to the tup that autumn

100 three-crop ewes 5.5 years old: to be put to the tup that autumn

100 four-crop ewes 6.5 years old: to be sold to a low ground farmer as they were getting too old to thrive on the hill

TOTAL STOCK – in summer: 960 including that season's lambs

in winter: 500

(These figures are theoretical and would vary greatly according to the season, the toll taken by disease and many other factors.)

Deaths – and these would be about 10% or more annually – would reduce the numbers in each age. Of the 180 ewe lambs marked, probably some 120, the very best, would be kept for stock replacement and would take the place of the 100 four-crop ewes that had been sold. The 60 smaller ewe lambs would be sold although, if the flockmaster was increasing his stock, he would keep the best of them as well.

Regular Aged Flocks

Under the system of regular ages in hill flocks each year sufficient ewe lambs were kept to match the numbers of cast ewes sold. This was the foundation on which these flocks were built. Each ewe lamb would be carefully marked at speaning by one or more lug marks cut into one of their ears. These lug marks were the permanent record of the year of birth, the hirsel and, sometimes, the flock to which that ewe lamb belonged. Indeed so good were the shepherds that one run through a race was all that was needed to shed out any sheep from another farm or one from a different hirsel and then get these safely penned away from the rest of the flock. This was always the first job to be done when the hirsel had been gathered into the fank. The flock was then aged by putting the flock down the race again and, by identifying the age mark on the sheep's ear, each age would be shed off and penned separately. 'The Book' could be then be filled in with an accurate and careful record of the numbers in each age. Some flocks used a brand on the face as the flockmark and the sheep would also be marked by the farm's buist with tar on the rib.

The only sheep coming on to the farm were occasional tups bought in from a neighbouring farm or from a stock where it was thought that an infusion of blood from that flock would be of benefit. The flock were therefore a closed stock and this had benefits in preventing infection and the transmission of diseases. A stock became acclimatised to that particular farm and this also minimised loss through disease. The alternative would be a flying flock where the farmer would buy in female stock each autumn, take a crop of lambs and then sell some or all of these ewes the following year. Such a system would be quite unworkable on the unfenced hills of Sutherland where the sheep stock was hefted.

Bound Stocks

These were sheep stocks legally bound to the land of that particular hill farm. When the flockmaster signed the lease for that farm he agreed to take over the existing sheep stock at an in-going valuation and, when he gave up the lease, to submit the stock to an out-going valuation. This ensured that, when a farm was going to become vacant, it could be advertised to let with a stock that was regular aged, acclimatised and hefted to that land. If the tenant saw to it that the stock was improved by good herding and careful breeding during his tenancy, then at waygoing, when he gave up his tenancy, the capital which he had invested would have increased. However, if during his tenancy the farmer had let the quality of that stock deteriorate, then he would receive less at waygoing than he had paid at the valuation when he went into the farm.

Wintering

The stock ewe lambs and the wether lambs (say 350 in total from that hirsel but about 1,750 hoggs – 5 x 350 – from a hill farm with five ewe hirsels) would go off to spend the winter on a lowground farm where the hill farmer had leased the 'wintering'. He would usually also send a 'hogg shepherd' to herd these until the following March when they would be driven home back to the hill farm. There the ewe hoggs would usually find and recognise their mothers. It was common to see a ewe with her lamb following her, followed by her last year's lamb, now a ewe hogg, and sometimes even by her previous year's lamb, now a maiden ewe. Following their mothers taught the next generation where to graze, where to cross the burns and generally how to make a certain part of the hirsel or heft their home.

The wether hoggs would go to one of the eild hirsels and were the replacements for the three-year-old wethers that had been sold at the last backend. This system of wintering worked well. It produced a better-grown hogg with fewer losses than if that hogg had been wintered at home. It reduced the mouths grazing the hirsel during the hungry months. In autumn, winter and spring there would be some 500 sheep grazing that hirsel but in summer there would be double that – maybe 960 to 1,000 sheep when the lambs are included.

Tup Lambs and Tups

The tup lambs, after speaning, were usually kept for the whole year on the arable fields around the farmhouse or sent away for wintering. They needed good feeding if they were to develop their potential. The number of tups required was about one tup to 40 ewes although often three tups per 100 ewes were kept in case of losses. Thus on a hill farm with five hirsels and a stock of 2000 ewes, some sixty tups would be kept and these would be in regular ages just like the ewes. The tups spent all the year in these fields at the farm apart from the weeks when they were out with the ewes, usually for about six weeks from late November to early January. At Eriboll the tups were kept for much of the year on Choraidh Island and there are still the ruins there of the bothy in which the shepherd, who herded the tups, lived while on the island. The tups were moved on and off the island by boat.

The tups were put out to a different hirsel from that on which they had been born to avoid inbreeding. There was a system on some farms whereby a group of especially fine ewes were drawn out and mated with a fine tup, often bought in from another flock. The tupping would be in an enclosed field at the farm. The purpose was to produce a batch of extra good young tups which would gradually improve the whole stock. This sometimes worked, especially when it was supervised by one of those elite flockmasters who had, 'an eye for a beast' and possessed the extraordinary ability to foresee the type of progeny that would result from the mating of a particular ewe with a particular tup.

This then was the system that obtained on the hill farms of Sutherland for some 150 years. There is little left there today of sheep or of men – just the shepherd's cottage, long since fallen down or sold as a holiday home.

13
Wool

Eriboll did flourish. The price of sheep and wool rose for the years from the 1840s to the 1870s. Imports of wool from Australia and lamb from New Zealand then began to have an adverse effect on prices in Scotland. The recorded prices which a farmer might have received for his wool clip and his Cheviot sheep in the years from 1840 to 1899 are as follows:

YEARS	*Cheviot Sheep*	*Cheviot Laid Wool*	*Cheviot White Wool*
1840–49	17s 11p	14s 0p	- -
1850–59	20s 3p	17s 5p	- -
1860–69	24s 5p	25s 3p	36s 4p
1870–79	29s 11p	22s 6p	32s 3p
1880–89	28s 2p	16s 10p	26s 9p
1890–99	22s 11p	13s 8p	21s 11p

Sheep prices are an average for wethers, ewes and lambs and then averaged again for the decade. Laid wool means wool from sheep that have been smeared. White wool means wool from sheep that have been dipped – not smeared. Wool prices are also the average of minimum and maximum price for each year and then averaged again for the decade.[62]

The 'Eild Clipping', which is the clipping of the sheep that did not breed that year, took place in early or mid-June. The 'Milk Clipping' of the ewes, which had lambs at foot, took place in late June or July. A rise comes in the wool in the early summer, when

62 Philip Gaskell, *Morvern Transformed*, 1968.

the fleece starts to separate from the sheep's body and hence that is the time to clip them. This occurs earlier in the season with eild sheep than it does with ewes. All the shepherds worked together to a pattern, gathering a hirsel in the early morning, clipping all day and returning the sheep to their hirsel in the evening. The next day it would be the turn of a neighbouring hirsel – unless it rained or the mist came down and so prevented the gather. This also caused problems for the wives making the meal and the accepted rule was, 'never start the cooking until you see them at the clipping'.

Wool was the backbone of Sutherland hill farming. The wool cheque paid the rent, by far the main expense in the trading year, and a bit more.

Smearing

The 'sundry expenses' for the year would include the cost of smearing of each sheep. Smearing of sheep goes back at least to the early 1800s. The work – and it was skilled work – was carried out by squads of contractors, often from Skye, who were paid by piece work for each sheep smeared. It was a valuable source of employment and hence cash for these squads. The catcher caught the sheep and placed it on a stool in front of the man doing the smearing. With one hand he then shedded or parted the fleece most carefully in rows from rump to neck and with the fingers of the other hand applied a mixture of warm Archangel tar and butter to the skin. He continued thus, shedding the wool and applying the tar and butter, working systematically until the whole fleece had been given its smearing. He then let it go and the catcher placed another sheep on the stool. The aim was for each man to smear twenty sheep each day. The Archangel tar and the butter were mixed and heated in a large cast iron cauldron over a fire, usually of peat, and then ladled out into small pots, which were placed near each stool. The operation normally took place inside a shed or building. The sheep had to be dry for the operation to be successful. The shepherds gathered in the sheep to the smearing shed and returned the smeared sheep back to their hirsels. All the rest of the work was done by the contractors. There is a smearing shed still standing on Forest Farm in Strath Chuilionaich, west of Ardgay.

Smearing was carried out in October or November each year before the tups were put out with the ewes. It was said to waterproof the fleece and to help to control lice, keds and other insects, which tend to infest sheep. It certainly waterproofed the fleece. I have been told that the sheep never throve so well in winter after smearing stopped and dipping came in. However, for the control of insects in the fleece and on the body of the sheep, there is no question but that dipping was far more effective. Also the quality of the wool improved greatly, hence the 20% to 25% higher price for white wool (from dipped sheep) than for laid wool (from smeared sheep).

Traces of the Archangel tar in the fleece from the smearing could not be scoured out and marked the finished woollen cloth with small black stains. When Australian wool began to be imported, the wool merchants were pleased to pay a premium for such wool as it could be guaranteed to have no tar stains. Hence dipping became established practice with far better control of keds and lice and soon of skin diseases such as sheep scab, which is caused by scab mites. Summer dipping followed, giving protection against fly strike by maggots. The practice of using tar with the branding iron to mark the sheep and to identify which farm the sheep belonged to also caused damage to the fleece. Later, marking fluids were introduced, which did not stain the wool and which would be scoured out during the cleaning process in the wool mill.

All sheep were washed before shearing. This entailed building a dam on a burn with a catching pen, often built of stone, on the bank alongside. On a dry day the sheep were gathered, shut in the pen and then caught and pushed into the burn one by one. They were made to swim round two or three times before climbing out. The grease, which was washed out of the fleece, would be carried down the burn leaving clean water to remove the grease from the next sheep. It was hard work and then the sheep needed a couple of dry days before being clipped. Clipping was easier and a little quicker with washed sheep. Washed wool received a higher price than greasy wool but weighed less. There appears to be the remains of a washing pool near where the burn enters Loch Eriboll beside the fank at Faoilinn. Washing of sheep continued until the middle of the twentieth century. The annual wool price schedule from the British Wool Marketing Board of those days showed separate prices for washed and greasy wool until the 1960s, when the washing of sheep was abandoned.

The wool was packed into long narrow wool sacks, which were hung up on a frame. A man climbed into the sack and then the rolled fleeces were thrown up to him to tramp in carefully. When lowered and sewn up, the wool sack was tight packed, regular and shapely. The flockmaster's name was stencilled on the sack along with a number. Great pride was taken in presenting the farm's wool clip to the wool merchant. At Eriboll the clip, perhaps about 150 wool sacks, was taken by rowing boat out to the trading ship, which was moored in the loch, and then stowed in the hold. There is a tale that on one occasion Alexander Clarke went out to the ship and found that the wool sacks had not been stowed with the wool sack numbers in sequence. He therefore ordered the whole of the Eriboll clip to be unloaded back into the rowing boat, taken ashore and sorted. The wool bags were then rowed back to the ship and stowed, this time in reverse order, so that, when the hatch covers were removed at Leith, the wool sack numbers would read from the top: 1, 2, 3, 4 and so on; downwards with the last number at the very bottom of the hold. Wool was the most valuable crop of the year. Things had to be done properly.[63]

63 Told to me by the late John Campbell, who was born at Arnaboll and whose family herded that hirsel.

The Wool Fair

From 1817 onwards the second Thursday in July each year was marked as the start of the Wool Fair held at the Plainstones in the town of Inverness. This great Fair, the annual meeting of all connected with sheep-farming in the Highlands, continued until the establishment of the auction marts around the latter half of that century. To the Wool Fair travelled all the flockmasters in the Highlands, many shepherds and drovers, plus the wool merchants, south country farmers and dealers from England. The factors also came to hear the gossip and to find out what was going on. The wool and the sheep were all sold unseen. The prices depended entirely on the recognised character and quality of the wool and the flock and the integrity of the flockmaster to deliver what he had promised. The flockmaster would make his round of the wool merchants and agree over the course of the week a price for the wool clip of that year. Similarly he would also make the rounds of the farmers and dealers from the south who had come to buy lambs and cast ewes; the lambs for wintering and resale in the spring and the ewes for crossing, usually with a Border Leicester tup. The numbers of sheep sold were vast. It is recorded that one farmer from the South regularly bought over 40,000 lambs each year at the Wool Fair. Arrangements would also be made for the droving and delivery of the sheep. This of course meant more bargaining with the drover who would agree to collect them from the farm of their birth and deliver them safely to the lowground farm. The sheep were all sold on the basis of so many clad score (a clad score being twenty-one sheep) and the number actually despatched would be twenty-one for each score. At that time the clad score was standard to any agreement for the sale of sheep and at the valuation of sheep stocks. Whether this extra of one per twenty was to cover loss on the journey from hill farm to destination is not known.

What a week of haggling there must have been! What discussions must have taken place in the taverns of an evening! Mitchell, the great civil engineer who followed Telford in road construction throughout the north, gives an excellent account of the Inverness Wool Fair in his book.[64] For several years after the Second World War, the name 'Wool Fair' was still given to the annual July sale of dairy cattle at Macdonald and Fraser's auction mart in Inverness, but all the bargaining and the week of the Wool Fair had come to an end with the development of the auction marts. In the auction ring the price was decided by the highest bid. The fall of the auctioneer's hammer ended all the arguments.

64 Joseph Mitchell, *Reminiscences of My Life in the Highlands*, Volume 1, 1884.

14

The Wintering of the Hoggs

It has long been recognised that hoggs need to be shifted off the hill farm on which they have been born and moved to different and better pastures for their first winter. The hoggs are the future of the flock. If they do not get a good wintering, they will not grow into sound and fitting replacements for the older sheep that will have been drafted and sold.

Away back in 1830, Patrick Sellar was writing in the *Farm Report* on his Strathnaver, Morvich and Culmaily farms how he had been suffering losses amongst his hoggs of between 15% and 30% from braxy and pining. He succeeded in reducing these losses by half and he did it by a programme of moving the lambs at speaning (weaning) to clean grazings on land which was derived from a different geology to that on which they had been reared. Thus, when the lambs were speaned, they were moved onto felspar land and, 'from that, if necessary, to the sandstone land at Culmaily'.[65]

Sellar is remembered for his notorious part in the Clearances but he was also a noted flockmaster, highly respected by his peers. He was regularly called on to advise on the art and practice of sheep husbandry in Sutherland. His advocacy of away wintering – the moving of ewe and wether hoggs to lowground farms for their first winter – was to become standard practice throughout the hill flocks of Sutherland and indeed standard practice throughout the Highlands. The grazing on the hill was too poor and the weather too rough for a lamb to grow into a good hogg during the first winter of its life but there was more to away wintering than that. The complete change of diet and trace elements gave a something

65 Patrick Sellar, *Farm Reports III County of Sutherland*, Library of Useful Knowledge, 1831.

to the hogg that is hard to describe. Even the droving, the long slow walk south in autumn and the return north in the spring, also gave a something to those hoggs; a hardiness and an ability to move. Away wintering also reduced the number of sheep grazing the hill farms almost by half during the winter months – the hungry season of the year.

At speaning time in August, the stock ewe lambs would first be drafted off and then the selling lambs. These would set out on the long walk to the sales, in earlier times straight to their new owner, and later to the auction sale at Lairg. From the hill farms in the north of the county this would take a week, with the shepherds sleeping out in the heather with their charges or, as they approached Lairg and the lambs were better settled, getting a bed for the night in a shepherd's house on Dalchork or elsewhere. After the sale it was the long walk back home for the shepherds, taking one day to cover the miles that had taken a week or more with the sale lambs. The keeping hoggs – ewe and wether, the future stock on that farm – would be drafted off and carefully selected, then lug marked and keeled and these would set out on the long walk to their wintering in Caithness or Easter Ross or the Black Isle. This droving would be undertaken by one of the farm's shepherds or sometimes by a wintering shepherd who worked for a wintering contractor.

These wintering contractors leased the grazings on lowground farms from September through to March and hired wintering shepherds, often young men seeking to learn the profession, to herd the hoggs through these months. Some of the larger flock-masters made bargains for the wintering direct with a lowground farmer. The terms agreed between winterer and farmer were strict. Payment had to be made to the farmer, half at the New Year and half when the hoggs went home. Often the farmer was required to provide board and lodging for the wintering shepherd. The farm must be clean, i.e. there must have been not a single sheep on that farm since the previous March. Most arable farms were then worked on a six or seven course rotation; lea oats, turnips, black ground oats or barley undersown with grass seeds, followed by three or four years in grass. There was therefore a wealth of mixed grazing available when the hoggs arrived and they got a good 'harvesting'. However the hoggs had to be off the young grass by the New Year and off the oldest grass by the end of January. That field or fields of old grass were then ploughed ready for the forthcoming crop of lea oats.

The hoggs would go on to the turnips in January but the needs of the cattle on the farm came first. Usually for every ten drills of turnip, eight would be clipped and carted off to feed the cattle with just two being left for the hoggs. The hoggs would also clean up the clipped turnip shaws, any small turnips left unclipped and the two drills which had been left for them. The wintering shepherd would control the hoggs by putting up breaks with nets and 'stickins' (light wooden posts). He would move his 'breaks' every week or so thus rationing out carefully the available turnip to see his hoggs through until the end of the winter. The bounty of the golden hoof of the hoggs would thus be spread right across the whole field that had grown the turnips. With a tool called a 'picker', the hogg shepherd would pick out all the turnip roots, which the hoggs had eaten down until only a shell with the tap root attached was left. This root was held to be the most valuable part of the turnip. The hoggs were only allowed on to the turnip for a set period each day, being turned in to the turnip first thing in the morning and then turned off again in the afternoon – always at precisely the same time – to a grass field or, better still, to a heather outrun if the farm was fortunate enough to possess such an asset. All the hoggs had to be off the lowground farm and on their way back to their hill farm by the end of March.

A good wintering was essential for the full growth of the hoggs' frame and their wool. Both ewe and wether hoggs had to go home well-grown and well-fleeced – not fat. Good away wintering brought out the best in them and caused them to thrive and grow when they returned to the hill. In earlier times they would go back to the hirsels where they had been reared. There they would usually find their mothers and settle down quickly to the grazing routine of that hirsel. Later, when many wether stocks had been dispersed due to the needs of the market and economics were demanding greater numbers of breeding ewes, the ewe hoggs were sent to an eild hirsel – high land which had formerly carried a wether stock. As described earlier, the poor hogg shepherd would then have the task of getting the hoggs to settle and spread out on this, to them, strange grazing, while all the time they wanted to return to the hirsel where they had been born or to that fine lowground farm where they had just spent the winter. They were even harder to settle if they had had too much turnip. They were then termed 'sweet mouthed' and it would take weeks and weeks of constant herding to get them settled. Meantime they lost much of the condition that they had gained while away. On some hill farms they would stay on the eild hirsel for a further year as maiden ewes, finally returning to their home hirsels in the back end of their second year. The task was then, once again, to get them settled.

Away wintering continued but changed with the coming of the railways in the second half of the nineteenth century, when the hoggs would be walked to Lairg station, loaded on to a special train and delivered to the down country station nearest to their wintering farm. There the wintering shepherd would take delivery of them and drive them to the lowground farm where they were to spend the winter. The next transport development was the coming of the stock lorry some years after the Second World War. This meant that the hoggs were now collected from their hill farm and delivered right to the field where they would start their wintering. By that time many arable farms in Easter Ross and elsewhere had started to keep their own flocks of breeding sheep; park sheep, first Half Breds and then North Country Cheviots. Fewer and fewer farms were now available for wintering the hoggs. In the second half of the twentieth century almost all arable farms abandoned the trusted system of the six or seven course rotation and turned to continuous cereal growing. Then the park sheep went and the fertiliser bag supplied the fertility. Fields and fields of barley, wheat and oil-seed rape formed the landscape of the arable lands. Fences were no longer maintained for there was no stock on the farms, and nor was there any need of men to herd them.

In the early years of the twenty-first century many of the hill flocks were dispersed or most seriously reduced. The glens and straths, which had been cleared of their tacksmen, subtenants and cattle to make room for the sheep two hundred years earlier, were now cleared of sheep. They became a vast, empty wilderness. For two centuries, every autumn thousands and thousands of hoggs had left their hill grazings and journeyed to lowground farms for wintering, and every spring those hoggs had returned to their hill grazing. It was prudent sheep husbandry but all that is no more. It is just a memory, especially for the men and their families who herded those sheep with diligence and skill.

15
The Herding of the Sheep

The arrival of the 'Great Sheep' with their attendant shepherds from the Borders set a completely new pattern for herding on the hills of Sutherland. The cattle of the old transhumant system would go. Sheep – Cheviots and Blackfaces – with their Border shepherds would take their place.

It was around 1790 that Sir John Sinclair of Ulbster, 'Agricultural Sir John' as he was known, established a flock of five hundred Cheviots under Border shepherds at Langwell in Caithness. Patrick Sellar was not far behind him. He had taken the lease of Strathnaver in 1814 and he also put his flocks, Cheviots, under the superintendence of Border shepherds. He writes:

> They were chiefly young men, who married and brought their sweethearts North with them. He [the writer] settled them in cottages on suitable parts of the farm; giving to each, where the situation admitted of it, a young man to board with them, in the manner agreed on with his tillage servants. The shepherds' wages, however, must exceed those given to ploughmen. If a shepherd does his duty, he must exercise a great deal of consideration, and must undergo much hardship; to which the man whose sleep is soundest in the wildest storm, and whose meat is regularly placed before him daily at certain hours, is not subjected. The householder is afforded a cottage and garden, thirteen bolls of meal, grass for three cows and one pony, with the profit to be gained from seventy Cheviot sheep of the different sorts each, mixed among the master's sheep of the same kind . . . The reporter, employing eleven married

shepherds and eight young men, this gives the number of twelve hundred and fifty shepherds' sheep or packs mingled among the master's flocks and spread over the farm; and thus, something like a partnership concern tacitly exists between master and servant; for, although the management rests entirely with the master and his managing shepherd, yet is every shepherd, old and young, deeply interested in the skill, prudence and vigour employed. And that master will prosper badly who does not hear, and patiently enquire into, all that every shepherd has to say, concerning each and every part of the management; taking due care as he goes on, as much as possible, to identify the interest of each with that of the whole community.[66]

Amen to that!

Mr Hall Dixon, 'a man with a great knowledge of the agricultural scene and the recently established great sheep runs' wrote around the mid-1860s:

Shepherds began at the age of 18, and serve a four or five year apprenticeship. At the end of that time, if they have become master shepherds, they have a cottage, grass for two cows and a horse and a pack of eighty sheep, or perhaps half a pack but a higher wage. The shepherd's pack would have a separate mark and his cast ewes went with the master's flock. The shepherd got a meal allowance of 61 bolls of meal [that is almost four tons of oatmeal] – and twice that if there was a lad in the house as it was a double herding, *i.e.* about 1000 ewes. He would have a couple of acres for some potatoes, oats and some turnip for the household, which made pot broth, often using a Ewe which had died of Braxy: It would be skinned, well

66 Patrick Sellar, *Farm Reports III County of Sutherland*, Library of Useful Knowledge, 1831.

pressed with stones in a burn, to extract the inflammation, then salted and hung. The main shepherding chores were at tupping and lambing time. The former saw him busy for six weeks, seeing that the sheep did not stray far from the tup, while lambing was the next busy period, lasting a month and usually beginning around the 18th of April.[67]

The flockmasters and their shepherds had many problems to face during those first decades of sheep farming in Sutherland. There were losses from theft. In earlier times the natives had looked on reiving – the practice of uplifting of stock from their neighbours – almost as a way of life, and now their descendants, the dispossessed small tenants, were not loath to help themselves to a sheep or two whenever there was an opportunity. In 1815 Patrick Sellar, with his usual determination and energy, combined with ten other flockmasters and the Marquess of Stafford to form 'The United Association of the Noblemen and Gentlemen in Sutherland and Caithness for the Protection of Property' to tackle this problem. Later they were joined by eleven flockmasters from Assynt and the Reay Country. The loss through theft was recorded as 1,591 sheep in 1815–16 but, during the next two years, the loss was 'beat down' to 853 and 754 respectively. Sellar also diligently pursued the policy of clearing any inhabitants who still remained in the hill country, down to the coast well away from the new sheep farms. A certain John Ross from Muie, Rogart, was tried for sheep stealing, found guilty and transported to Australia. Shepherds were required to keep watch for sheep stealers and the Association paid premiums to those shepherds who had been successful in reducing the black loss on their hirsel.

There were losses through disease. The sheep throve on those clean pastures but there were big losses among the hoggs through braxy and pining. Sellar states, 'the loss seldom fell short of fifteen per cent, and varied between that and thirty'.

67 Hall Dixon, *Observations of a Traveller, c.* 1860.

He evolved a system of moving the hoggs on to hirsels with a different underlying geology before sending them on down to the lowground. He continues, 'By a vigilant attention to these measures the losses on the farm were reduced nearly one half, and the stock exhibited a greater degree of health.'[68] Today braxy is controlled by injection but it is remembered as a disease which usually afflicted hoggs that were really thriving. This fits in with the picture of sheep stocks doing well on grazings which had never before been grazed by a flock of sheep. The same benefit from clean ground may apply to diseases associated with ticks ,for there is no mention of tick-borne fever, nor of lamb cripples. It could just be that the previous transhumant cattle husbandry had not allowed the ticks to thrive but, in the distant future, ticks would be a problem – and a very serious one. Pining is now controlled by dosing with cobalt.

There were various black losses. These were losses which could not be accounted for, such as drowning, being lost in bogs and theft. To arrive at the total number of sheep which should be present on the hirsel at the annual reckoning, the number of lambs which had been marked had to be added to the total and the number of sheep which had been sold deducted. The skins of any sheep that had died had to be produced by the shepherd. If the total did not tally with the count of the sheep present on the hirsel, then the shortfall was called 'black loss'.

In Allan Fraser's novel, *Fiddler's Doom*, the story is related of the factor going over with the shepherd the count of the sheep on his hirsel. The shepherd says to the factor:

'And would you be wishing to take a look through the sheep now that you are here, sir?'

'No need for that, Campbell, I have the figures. You'll let me know if you come on those missing ewes?'

68 Patrick Sellar, *Farm Reports III County of Sutherland*, Library of Useful Knowledge, 1831.

'Indeed yes, sir. I'll be sending the boy here running all the way to Dunblair Castle if we should come on a horn.'

Mr Scott's face grew a deeper red at this remark. He realised the impudence behind the courtesy. But, as he was fond of saying, the hand that signs the cheque rules. He said: 'You understand that if you can't account for missing sheep, their value comes off your wages, Campbell.'

'Indeed yes, sir, that was always the way of it wherever I was herd. Except in one place, sir, where the gentleman himself managed his own affairs.'

Mr Scott took no notice of the insult, or perhaps he did not notice it.[69]

There were losses from predation by foxes, eagles and others. Foxhunters were employed to deal with this. They were paid (in 1819) £15 per annum plus twenty-six and a half bolls of meal (which is just over 1.5 tons), a cottage, land sufficient for a cow, a potato patch and a right to cut peats. The foxhunter was required to have ten or more dogs – four foxhounds, two lurchers and four terriers. He also received a bounty on his kill thus:

Pair of fox's ears	10/-
Bitch (vixen) in milk	10/-
Cub	5/-
Wild Cat	5/-
Martin or Polecat	3/6
Talons of adult Eagle	15/-
Head and Talons of Raven	2/6
Head and Talons of Hawk	1/-
Head of Magpie or Crow	6p
Head of young Crow	1p

69 Allan Fraser, *Fiddler's Doom*, 1939.

It was a job that suited those native to Sutherland fine, for it was hunting and the foxhunter was left on his own to get on with it. There was a foxhunter at Muiseal in Strathmore, employed jointly by the Clarkes at Eriboll and others. When sport became important during the second half of the 1800s, it was from the foxhunters that the first stalkers and gamekeepers were recruited. They were most highly skilled in their trade.

The life of a shepherd was the welfare of the sheep. Whether it was storm or theft or disease or any other matter affecting the life of his flock, the shepherd gave of his all to the sheep in his charge. It was indeed a hard life but yet a satisfying one. The daily routine was 'to lift the ewes off the greens' at the same time every afternoon, usually three o'clock, and move them up to the higher ground where they would spend the night. They would move steadily upwards along the sheep tracks in single file forming long lines of sheep, white against the dark background of heather and heath. 'Lift your ewes off the greens at the same time every afternoon' was the first rule in herding. It applied to every hirsel – ewe or wether. The second rule was, 'Never use a dog unless you have to.' If you kept to a regular routine and to a regular timetable, the sheep would not need a dog. The sheep responded to a regular timetable – and still do. They needed little persuasion to make that daily journey up to the higher ground in the afternoon and down again in the morning; one whistle and they would all start to move. It is natural for a sheep to seek the higher ground in the evening, maybe because of some inbred instinct that predators can be more readily seen from the higher slopes. This movement also gave the sheep a mixed diet. The grasses and herbs from the greens, from along the burns and from the shielings, which had been grazed during the day, were added to the heather and roughage from the higher ground grazed during the evening. This gave the sheep a mixture in their stomachs on which to chew the cud contentedly during the night. It also kept the greens clean, for the greater portion of the dung would be passed during the night high up on the hill. In the early morning the shepherd would walk the tops, turning the sheep down to the lower ground once again.

There is a pastoral parallel here with the deer and the wolf. Frank Fraser Darling in *The Pelican in the Wilderness* tells of his travels through the United States of America studying the land use and the people. He relates how he kept on coming across situations common to the U.S.A. and to the Highlands of Scotland. He writes:

> It was here [Wisconsin], and later in Utah, that I got the idea of how important the wolf was in the well-being of the land. The wolf keeps the deer on the move, whatever their species and one of the lessons of life I have learned about herbivorous animals is that they must be kept moving. Then my mind played on our own sheep pastoralism in Scotland. Because we have no wolf we can use a breed of sheep which grazes in a dispersed state of twos and threes rather than as a closed flock, but nevertheless the Mountain Blackface sheep still tends to overgraze and soil the green patches alongside the rivers and green talus slopes on the hills. The good shepherd keeps his sheep on the move and to this end has developed an artificial wolf in the collie dog which not only gathers but drives as well. Each evening the good shepherd walks up the glen with his driving dog, putting the sheep up the hillsides.[70]

There was also the herding of the sheep at different seasons of the year onto different parts of the hirsel. They would be kept on the very barest ground after speaning to put the milk off them. In February and March they would be given a certain time each day to graze on the draw moss, the cotton grass. In spring they would be kept off the best of the greens to save these for the lambing.

70 Frank Fraser Darling, *Pelican in the Wilderness*, 1956.

It was a form of pasture control and management, developed by years of patient observation. Where the shepherd herded his hirsel well, his sheep could be seen to be content and thriving.

Again, in *Fiddler's Doom* Allan Fraser tells of herding and of Archie Campbell, the Argyll shepherd, telling the boy, Alicky, the ways of his sheep.

The shepherd knew where each heft of sheep would be found. He knew too each sheep as a man will know his acquaintances in a village. He knew their faces, and their history, their parentage, peculiarities and behaviour.

He would point his stick at a lean ewe, saying to Alicky: 'Aye, it's herself that's the lean one. She's been like that in the spring for the last three years. You would be thinking, indeed, that it was fluke that was to do with her, but never yet has she been poked [a swelling under the jaw, a sign that the sheep's liver has been invaded by fluke] below the jaw as a fluky sheep will always be. And the last three years, though you'd be thinking it's eild that she was by the look of her, she would have as bonny a lamb at her foot as any ewe on the heft, aye, and milk it well.'

He would point his stick at another, saying: 'Aye, she's a good ewe indeed as her mither was and her granny were before her. She would never be leaving a lamb that wasn't a top. But it's a fair bit of grazing she would have as her gang.'

Again, he would point to a strong and heavy wether. 'It is the bold one that's in it, indeed. He would have been away two years back, but I will be keeping him on a whiley yet, for there's no drift of snow that he's not fit to break through, and the weak yowes following behind him. Aye, and he's the bold strong sheep he is indeed and after the best tup we ever had on the place.'[71]

71 Allan Fraser, *Fiddler's Doom*, 1939.

The shepherd's wife was a most important part of the life on the hirsel. There was the isolation. It was a lonely and often anxious life for her when the shepherd would be out on the hill whatever the weather during all the hours of daylight and sometimes into the hours of darkness too. I have heard it said that it was not considered right for a shepherd to be inside his house during the hours of daylight. There was the need to have a meal ready for him at whatever hour he might come in. There were the children to be brought up and the cow to be milked and tended. There was the work of carrying the water from the well, the making of the hay, the cutting the peats and much else besides. Then there were the handlings – the markings, the clippings and the dippings – when all the neighbouring shepherds had to be fed and well fed at that.

The shepherd would be dressed in a suit of homespun tweed with stockings which they had knitted themselves as they watched over the flock. They carried a plaid as a protection against the cold and wet in the days before the waterproof 'Mackintosh' was invented. The plaids were homespun and were 'about three-and-a-half yards long, including the fringe, with border at each end'. They wore heavy hobnailed boots, often of horsehide, the toes of which turned up with age. The bonnet on the head and the stick in the hand completed the outfit. Shepherds kept to the same steady long striding pace on the brae as they kept on the flat, uphill and downhill, and they maintained it from dawn to dusk. They were a remarkable race of hardy, responsible men and women, whose work was their life and whose life was their sheep.

16
Trenching

Apart from the oceans, our food all comes from the soil of those parts of the planet where crops can be grown or domestic animals grazed. Ever since man started to settle down as a farmer, he has broken in and reclaimed land from a state of nature to one capable of growing his crops. The most accessible and naturally fertile land was chosen first. As the population grew and the demand for food increased, the reclamation of more difficult sites became necessary.

By the early 1800s trenching was the method which had developed to bring moorland into cultivation. It was akin to what a gardener might call double digging. The turf was first skimmed off. The top spit, which was roughly a spade's depth of soil, was then dug out and turf and top spit were set aside. The now exposed subsoil was then broken up to a depth of at least a further spit. The turf was then inverted, placed on top of the disturbed subsoil and the top spit of soil replaced on top of the turf. The soil profile of that potential arable land was now from the bottom up: first, free draining subsoil, then decaying turf and on top of that friable topsoil. The breaking up of the subsoil was particularly important as it destroyed any indurated layer that had been present and which would have restricted both drainage and root growth. And so across the moors, furrow after furrow was dug in this way – trenched – to create so many of the fields that we farm today. It was back-breaking work.

The result of good trenching right across a moor was the creation of a field with the potential of being capable of growing arable crops. The soil of that field now had six to nine inches of topsoil overlying the decaying inverted turf and this lay on top of the broken up subsoil. This soil now needed lime to correct its acidity and then dung, which would decay along with the turf. The addition of this lime and this dung brought that soil into an improving state which would provide the nutrients for the growth of the host of earthworms and other invertebrates, which are the very basis of a fertile soil. There must then follow years and years of more lime, more dung and the continuous rotation of crops to create the productive fields that we have inherited today. Omit adding lime and dung, omit the rotation of crops and the careful husbandry and that land will revert to an ugly and unproductive field.

J. A. Symon records that, 'On the Ross-shire estate of Ardross no fewer than 2600 acres were reclaimed by trenching, draining and liming in nine years from about 1850. New steadings were erected; 67.5 miles of stone dykes were built and 3000 acres were enclosed for planting. All these operations were carried out by the proprietor.'[72] The pattern for this activity had been set out twenty years earlier by John Baigrie. In his essay, *Description of a Farm in the Western Extremity of Eastern Ross, Ross-shire,*[73] John Baigrie first describes the size of the farm and the deplorable state that it was in when he first gained entry in 1825. He goes on to outline the steps that he took to set out the farm in fields of twelve to twenty-five acres. He then describes the operations carried out under four headings: Draining, Blasting Stones, Trenching and Fences.

'As draining was evidently the first necessary operation, a number of labourers were employed for that purpose, who executed the work by the job or piece.' After detailing the depth of the drains and how they were built with small stones gathered from the land, he gives the cost of this work as three pence per lineal ell

72 W. Mackenzie, *Report on Improvements at Ardross.* Referred to by J. A. Symon in *Scottish Farming Past and Present,* 1959.
73 John Baigrie, *Farm Reports Description of a Farm in the Western Extremity of Eastern Ross,* Library of Useful Knowledge, 1831.

of thirty-seven inches and how a skilled labourer could earn for himself two shillings to half-a-crown a day for this work. The fields were then trenched with a spade to a depth of sixteen inches. The labourers were paid fourteen pounds per acre for this work, which was reduced to eleven pounds per acre if there was no brushwood to be cleared first. The smaller stones were gathered and used to form the drains. The large boulders were left for blasting.

Blasting the larger stones and boulders was paid for at fifteen pence per foot of bore. That bore was made by a steel jumper (a round steel chisel about three feet long) being held in the hole and turned by one man while his mate gave that jumper repeated blows with a hammer. Black powder was then rammed into the bore and fired to split the boulder. Many required thirty feet of bore to produce stones of a size suitable for building the dykes. Baigrie then describes the building of the fences (stone dykes). These were some size. They were three feet wide at the base and rose to an overall height of five feet four inches. The payment for building these stone dykes was sixpence per ell with extra being paid for carting in the stones. Alongside the new dyke a ditch was cut, which was seven feet wide at the top and three and a half feet deep. Baigrie then goes on to describe the liming, the rotation of crops and the growing of turnips and wheat and oats.

Baigrie's close attention to detail stands out as does the care with which all the operations for the betterment of the land were carried out. Good crops of turnips meant more cattle and more sheep being kept and thus more dung to enrich the land. Ardross must been a hive of activity while all this was underway. Driving through Ardross on the Struie Road (B9176) today, with fields of wheat and barley stretching out on both sides of that road and away on to the west, the landscape shows clearly just what John Baigrie and those who followed after him have accomplished.

All this my great grandfather, Alexander Clarke (1802–1877), and my grandfather, George Granville Clarke (1833– 1909), must have seen in its early stages when they drove over the Struie. They would also have read and studied Baigrie's essay in that copy of the volume, published by The Society for the Diffusion of Useful Knowledge, which I have inherited from them. They were determined, both of them, to put all this into practice on the unimproved land around the fields of Eriboll.

The 2nd Duke of Sutherland bought Ardross estate in 1834 and sold it again in 1843. He must have seen the smiling arable fields which his tenant, John Baigrie, had a little earlier created out of what had been exhausted, primitive farmland. Maybe the Duke told his son, the 3rd Duke, the story of those fields and maybe, just maybe, all this came to mind when the 3rd Duke started to plan the reclamations at Shinness, near Lairg. There is still a reminder of the short ownership of Ardross by the Duke of Sutherland in the farm name 'Stittenham', which lies beside the Struie Road as that road leaves the arable lands and heads out northwards into the forests and moors. Across the road there is also Stittenham House which is said to have been built by the Duke as an inn for travellers on the lines of the Moine House and the Crask Inn in Sutherland. Stittenham is a place name associated with the Dukes of Sutherland and their estates in England.

There is also a series of letters on the reclamation of land for growing turnip from Alexander and then from George Granville Clarke, first to James Loch and later to his son, George Loch, who were both commissioners for the Duke of Sutherland's estates.[74] This correspondence starts with a 1,400 word treatise by Alexander, dated 15 March 1847, on the need to grow turnips as winter feed for sheep in the county of Sutherland. Alexander points out that it was the availability of forage in the winter which limited the number of sheep that the sheep farms of Sutherland could carry. If more turnips could be grown at home for winter feed, then these hill farms would be able to carry far more sheep throughout the year. Further, the costs of moving the hoggs and 'the weak end of the flock' to and from the arable farms of Easter

74 National Library of Scotland, *Sutherland Collection.*

Ross or Caithness in the autumn and back in the spring plus the cost of renting the winter keep there would be saved. Alexander goes on to say that he 'had considerable experience of cultivation, tho' on a small scale, having improved and enclosed nearly 100 acres' at his own expense.

In 1858 Alexander sets out his proposals for an extension of his lease for another nineteen years, whereby the estate would provide the capital, 'to extend to as many acres as will, with that now in cultivation, make the whole arable land 250 acres – (which would give 50 acres of turnip under a five course shift) or 300 acres, if so much can be got for improvement contiguous. Five per centum per annum to be paid [by the tenant] for the actual outlay in trenching, draining and dyking.' There is also correspondence between George Loch, commissioner, and John Crawford, factor at Tongue, on the matter.

Loch did agree with this general concept but sounded the warning that there must be an adequate return for the estate on the capital that would have to be spent. Alexander did secure agreement to his proposal that land should be reclaimed from the outrun at Eriboll and brought into cultivation and this was written into the next renewal of his lease of Eriboll. However it was his son, George Granville, who was granted the go-ahead for a much more ambitious programme of land reclamation there, and this was to be backed up with building stabling for more horses and cottages for the ploughmen plus a new threshing mill with the necessary mill lades and mill wheel. All this went ahead.

The first Ordnance Survey of 1874 seems to show that trenching was actually in progress on the ridge to the north of the steading at Eriboll when that survey was being carried out. There is oral evidence that the women from Laid were ferried across the loch each morning to gather the stones on the newly reclaimed land.[75] The result of that stone gathering is still there today in the huge

75 Told to me by the late John Campbell, whose family herded Arnaboll for many years.

mounds of stones lying alongside the road to the shore. All this would not have been agreed without some right hard bargaining between George Granvillle Clarke, as tenant, and John Crawford, as the local factor. However agreed it was and the results stand out on Eriboll today.

The reclamation at Eriboll took place against a background of the 3rd Duke of Sutherland's drive and enthusiasm for his steam ploughs and for ever more acres of reclamation at Shinness and elsewhere. Dr Tindley in her book, *The Sutherland Estate, 1850–1920: Aristocratic Decline, Estate Management and Land Reform*,[76] describes well the eight Fowler steam plough sets in action at Shinness. These were ploughing a furrow two feet deep and subsoiling below that with 'The Duke's Toothpick'. It was claimed that, 'they needed a coalmine in front of them and a river of water behind them in the field where they were at work' plus an army of some hundred men to keep those steam engines working. In four years 1,829 acres were reclaimed. It was all costing a great deal of the Duke's money, some say around £180,000. However when describing the Duke's reclamations John R. Allan writes: 'The spectacle cost the Duke a pretty penny but there is no point in being a duke if you can't have fun'.[77] The reclamation with the steam plough sets continued but on a much smaller scale at Badanloch, Achentoul and Ribigill.

By the early 1880s, however, the 3rd Duke's enthusiasm for his reclamations was waning. These were not the agricultural nor the scientific successes that he had expected. Around 1879 there had also been a serious fall in the prices for sheep, wool and other farm produce and this marked the end of a very profitable period for sheep farming. It proved difficult to find applicants willing to take on the tenancies of these newly created farms. Thereafter perhaps too little care was taken of much of the reclaimed land

76 Annie Tindley, *The Sutherland Estate, 1850–1920: Aristocratic Decline, Estate Management and Land Reform*, 2010.
77 John R. Allan, *North-East Lowlands of Scotland*, 1952.

at Shinness; no applications of dung and no rotation of crops. Much reverted to its earlier state. At Badanloch, Ribigill and part of Achentoul the reclaimed land must have been looked after better, for today it is still carrying a reasonable sole of grass. John Baigrie's trenched land at Ardross is growing barley and wheat while my grandfather's trenched land at Eriboll is growing productive pasture.

It is the farmer's hand and the farmer's foot that are needed when it comes to building up the fertility in newly reclaimed land and then keeping that land in good heart. The factors whom the 3rd Duke of Sutherland employed did not possess the enthusiasm or the commitment to see that the rules of good husbandry were applied. The countryside will only blossom and yield her increase when the art and practice of good husbandry is faithfully and diligently applied. The soil is our heritage.

17

The Land

They have made my pleasant portion a desolate wilderness.
They have made it desolate, and being desolate it mourneth
unto me; the whole land is made desolate because no man
layeth it to his heart.

Jeremiah XII vv.10 (part) and 11.

The destiny of the human race is bound up with the land. What
of that land? The hill lands of Sutherland have gone back over the
past two hundred years. We have allowed those mountains and
moorlands to deteriorate into what Frank Fraser Darling described
sixty years ago in *West Highland Survey*[78] as a devastated terrain.
In his foreword to that book he wrote: 'And, finally, the bald
unpalatable fact is emphasised that the Highlands and Islands are
largely a devastated terrain' and he continued, '. . . and any policy
which ignores this fact cannot hope to achieve rehabilitation'.
We have ignored this fact. We have done nothing to rehabilitate
that countryside.

The land has indeed gone back. The Highlands and Islands
were once productive. There is sound evidence for this. During
the years centred around 1790, the mountains and moorlands in
that part of Scotland were grazing every summer some 500,000
cattle plus other stock. Some 70,000 of those cattle were being
exported south annually. And, in 1794, the Sutherland countryside produced eight hundred recruits for the Reay Fencibles, all
within a fortnight of the call to enlist and all of them passed as fit
for military service. These were not starving peasants. They were
fit young men who were to give valiant service during their years

78 Frank Fraser Darling, *West Highland Survey*, Oxford University Press, 1955.

in the Fencibles. And, in the 1920s, Eriboll was producing a bag of around four hundred brace of grouse every season. There is a photograph of my father with a basket of ten large trout taken from one of the hill lochs there in just one afternoon's fishing. And again, in 1921 at the time of the Clarke's waygoing, Eriboll was carrying a stock of 5,118 sheep plus lambs. The 2,607 ewes had lambed 2,343 lambs, a lambing percentage of around 80% to 90% and that without any hand-feeding whatsoever. The mountains and moorlands of Sutherland were once productive countryside.

The decline has been slow. In the 1870s sheep-farming was the major industry in Sutherland and was about to enter a period of economic depression. James Macdonald was writing:

> Some of the sheep farmers are beginning to find that their farms will not carry so many sheep, nor keep them in such high condition, as fifteen or twenty years ago. Considerable portions of the grazings are becoming foggy* and rough and of little value as sheep pasture . . . The cause of this we believe is the covering of the land over so long a period exclusively with sheep, without any Highland cattle being allowed upon it, as was the case before sheep-farming reached its height.[79]

> [* foggy: Instead of pastures being green and leafy, they had become grey and lifeless.]

Despite all the careful management of the flockmasters and the diligent herding of their shepherds, the grazings were going back. The rich variety of sweet grasses, herbs and clovers of the shielings, which had been inherited from the transhumant husbandry of the cattle, was replaced by heather and deer's hair and bracken. Muirburn was now being regularly practised on the grazings and

79 J. Macdonald, *Transactions of the Highland and Agricultural Society of Scotland*, 1880.

the sheep were continually defoliating and weakening each and every edible plant.

On the hills of Sutherland the generous sweep of the cow's tongue had been replaced by the sheep's selective nibble. The cow is a general grazer. While she will not eat perennial weeds like dockens and thistles, she grazes the grasses and herbs by sweeping them into her mouth with her tongue and then cutting these off by closing her teeth against her upper dental pad. Her digestive system then breaks it all down, extracts the nutritive portion and returns the rest to the land in her dung. She profits the land in two ways. Her method of grazing gathers both fine and rough herbage, thus improving the sward. Then she drops her dung back onto the land where it breaks down, feeding the insects and feeding the soil. The sheep on the other hand is selective. She picks the finest grasses and herbs, the choicest available, and bites them off. Like the cow, her digestive system also breaks it all down, extracts the nutritive portion and returns the rest to the land, but her dung does not seem to possess the rich beneficial qualities of the cow's dung.

The generous grazing of many cows and the selective bite of a few sheep are both needed to establish and maintain fine pasture. In the natural world all grazing systems have a variety of animals to harvest the herbage. In Sutherland the mixed summer grazing of former years by cattle with a few sheep, goats and ponies was changed to an all the year-round defoliation by a single species – sheep. There were very few red deer in those days. The mixed grazing of this transhumant pastoral husbandry created a diversity of plants in the sward and an increase in the fertility of the soil. The continuous single species grazing by sheep slowly destroyed that store of wealth. It was not so much the sheep which did the damage but the system under which they were kept. The one-time rich pastures of the Romney Marsh and of the Canterbury Plains of New Zealand were established and maintained by being grazed solely by sheep. However the grazing of these pastures was strictly controlled and it was managed with knowledge and great skill. On the unfenced hills of Sutherland the diligent daily herding by the shepherds was not sufficient to give full control of the grazing and so prevent the slow rundown of the quality of those pastures and the fertility of the soil. The hills of Sutherland needed and still need most careful pastoral husbandry. They did not get it under the management of the flockmasters.

There is further evidence of the decline in the well-being of the hill land over the past hundred and fifty years in the game books that were kept in the Highland shooting lodges. They tell of bags of grouse which are quite unobtainable today and of a variety of species shot that is now unbelievable. Even twenty-five years ago I can remember lambing at Edderton to the piping of the golden plover, the tumbling display flights of the peewit and the warning call of the cock grouse. Today the call of the moorland birds is muted if not totally silent, and every hill man over the age of fifty will tell the same tale.

The number of worms, beetles and other organisms which live within the topsoil is an indication of the well-being of that topsoil; that 6 inches to 9 inches of earth, which covers most of the habitable areas of our planet. Soil scientists call this topsoil the 'A Horizon' of the soil profile. All our food – apart from fish – and all our timber is produced from that A Horizon. Even many freshwater fish are dependent on clean, nutrient-rich water and they will not thrive if we allow life within the A Horizon to decline. The future of human life on this earth depends on the wellbeing of that shallow six to ten inches or so of soil.

The future wellbeing of all life on earth depends on our care of the topsoil – that shallow but vital layer of soil. There is within nature an ability to improve the soil. Had we seen the state of the land as it emerged from under its icy covering at the end of the Ice Age, we could never have foreseen that, within the space of several thousand years, the lower land would be growing a forest, which would in time support a far greater range of wildlife than we know today. The colonising of that early post glacial landscape – bare, desolate and uninviting – would have been started with wind-blown seeds developing into small mosses, annuals and herbs to be followed by dwarf shrubs, willow and birch, and from these to boreal forest. The leaf fall, the work of the earthworms and the circulation of nutrients all worked together to build a soil out of the raw debris left by the ice sheet. Life in all its forms built on these newly formed soils and, in turn, slowly created deeper and more fertile soils. Much later man worked these soils to grow his crops. As the centuries passed he developed the knowledge and skill to add to the fertility of that topsoil. On the cropped land man used the plough, the dung, the lime, the rotation of crops, the clover and the golden hoof of the folded flock to add to the depth and richness of that A Horizon. On the hills and uplands man's transhumant system of summer grazing by cattle with other livestock increased the fertility of those poor shallow soils.

Sometimes we stop using practices of husbandry which are beneficial, and we change to ways which impoverish the soil. These damage the wellbeing of the soil and thus bring harm to all life, including man. Such damage the Clarkes and other flock-masters in Sutherland inflicted on their sheep runs over a period of a century and a half. No serious steps have yet been taken to rebuild the fertility of the soil of these mountains and moorlands.

I would close this account of the Clarke family and their sheep husbandry with yet another two quotations.

The first is from the book by the late Professor W. H. Pearsall in the *New Naturalist* Series. He writes in his introduction:

There is another Britain, to many of us the better half, a land of mountains and moorlands and of sun and cloud, and it is with this upland Britain that these pages are concerned. It is equal in area to lowland Britain but its population is less than that of a single large town. It lies now as always beyond the margins our industrial and urban civilisations, fading into the western mists and washed by northern seas, its needs forgotten and its possibilities almost unknown.[80]

And the second is from the Old Testament, from the Book of the Prophet Ezekiel, Chapter XXXVI, vv. 34 and 35 (part):

. . . and the desolate land shall be tilled, whereas it lay desolate in the sight of all that passed by. And they shall say, this land that was desolate is become like the garden of Eden.

I would say 'Amen' to that.

80 W. H. Pearsall, *Mountains and Moorlands*, Collins, London 1950.

Glossary

Ewe lamb: Female lamb from birth (mid-April/early May) to speaning [weaning] (late July/early August).

Tup lamb: Male lamb (not castrated) from birth to speaning (dates as above).

Wether lamb: Male lamb (after castration at c14 days) from castration to speaning (dates as above).

Ewe hogg: Female sheep from speaning (July/Aug) to first clipping (June/July).

Tup hogg: Male sheep (entire) from speaning to its first clipping (dates as above).

Wether hogg: Male sheep (castrated) from speaning to its first clipping (dates as above).

Gimmer: Female sheep from its first to its second clipping.

Shearling or Dinmont: Male sheep (entire) from its first to its second clipping; thereafter two-shear tup, three-shear tup, etc.

Wether: Male sheep (castrated) from its first to its second clipping; thereafter two year old wether, three year old wether, etc.

Maiden ewe: A ewe from its second to its third clipping, which has not been put to the tup; thereafter, from giving birth to a lamb, she becomes a one-crop ewe, two-crop ewe, etc.

Ewe: Female sheep of breeding age. On hill farms she drops her first lamb at three years old; on better farms at two years old.

185

Grit ewe: Pregnant ewe.

Keb ewe: A ewe that has lost her lamb.

Eild ewe: A ewe that is not (or has not been) carrying a lamb.

Draft ewe: A ewe, after usually four crops of lambs, sold off to a lowground farm.

Correct ewe: Draft ewe, sold guaranteed correct in mouth and udder.

Broken-mouthed ewe: A ewe that has lost one or more of its teeth.

Bad-uddered ewe: A ewe that has got a faulty udder.

Tup: Ram. Male sheep (entire) expressly kept for breeding.

Rigg: Male sheep, usually a lamb, which has only one testicle.

FLOCK

Regular aged and bound stocks: See text in Chapter 12.

Score: Twenty sheep. Often used in the count of a flock; e.g. four and a half score would be ninety sheep.

Clad score: Twenty-one sheep. The clad score was always used in bargain in former times.

Shott: The smallest and poorest sheep in any lot.

Ewe hirsel: Area of a hill farm with its own regular aged ewe stock and shepherd.

Eild hirsel: Area of a hill farm with its own stock of wethers and shepherd – later stocked with gimmers and/or maiden ewes and/or wethers.

Heft: A part of a hirsel, occupied as their home by a certain number of ewes and their followers. A hirsel is made up of a series of hefts.

Hefted: An instinct in a sheep to stay on its heft acquired by a ewe, or a wether, and achieved by constant herding by the shepherd.

HANDLING

Stell: A circular enclosure, formed by a round stone dyke, maybe 15 to 20 yards in diameter, into which a cut of sheep could be shut before or during a snowstorm. Even in the worst snow storm, stells never filled with snow.

Fank: A collection of pens, originally built of stone dykes, latterly of wooden post and rail construction, for holding and sorting sheep.

Race: A narrow passage, the width of one sheep, in a fank.

Shedder: A narrow gate fitted into the side of the race, by which sheep can be sorted.

Buist: An identifying mark on the wool of a sheep, originally using hot tar.

Buisting iron: A hand tool with a letter, depicting the farm name, attached to a short handle for marking a sheep (buisting) with an identifying mark.

Keeled: A distinguishing mark, made by a mixture of coloured chalk and oil, applied at the exact same place on every sheep in that lot.

Lug mark: A cut or small nick made in a sheep's ear to record its year of birth, its sex, its hirsel and sometimes its farm.

Smearing: Applying a mixture of butter and Stockholm tar to the fleece of sheep in the autumn to provide waterproofing and maybe some protection against skin parasites. Smearing was superseded by dipping.

Dipping: Submerging sheep in a dipping bath filled with sheep dip to give protection against parasites and certain diseases of the skin.

MISCELLANEOUS

Tacksman: A man who held the 'tack' (lease) of a farm from the clan chief and then rented that land out to a number of subtenants in return for a proportion of the crop grown and other labour e.g. cutting and carting his peats, etc.

Flockmaster: The owner and manager of a flock (usually large) of hill sheep.

Run rig: An early system of cultivation of arable land whereby a characteristic ridge and furrow pattern was created, the crop being planted on the ridge and the furrow acting as a drain. Allocated annually by lot among the subtenants so that each would have both good and poor rigs.

Crop rotation: The growing of a regular succession of crops and grass whereby each field on an arable farm increased in fertility and achieved some weed control. The seven year rotation would be: lea oats, turnips, barley or oats under-sown with grass seeds, followed by four years in grass. Many Scottish estates required their tenants to keep strictly to this rotation and so secure the fertility and freedom from weeds of that farm.

A Farm in good heart: A well-farmed holding, increasing in fertility and free of weeds.

Bibliography

Adam, R.J. (ed), *John Home's Survey of Assynt*, T. & A. Constable, Edinburgh, 1960

Advisory Panel on the Highlands and Islands, *Land Use in the Highlands and Islands*, HMSO, Edinburgh, 1964

Baigrie, John, *Description of a Farm in the Western Extremity of Eastern Ross*, Library of Useful Knowledge, 1831

Beake, Lesley, *Merino*, Maskew Miller Longman Pty Ltd., Cape Town, 1989

Bangor-Jones, Malcolm, 'The Coming of the Great Sheep', *The Northern Times*, Golspie, 1988

Bangor-Jones, Malcolm, 'Sheep Farming in Sutherland in the Eighteenth Century', *The Agricultural History Review*, Vol 50, Part II, 2002

Daniell, William, *Daniell's Scotland. A Voyage round the Coast of Scotland and the adjacent Isles 1815–1822*. Volume I. Birlinn, Edinburgh, 2006

Darling, F. Fraser, *Island Years*, G. Bell and Sons, 1940

Darling, F. Fraser, *Island Farm*, G. Bell and Sons, 1943

Darling, F. Fraser, *West Highland Survey*, Oxford University Press, 1955

Darling, F. Fraser, *Pelican in the Wilderness*, George Allen & Unwin Ltd, London, 1956

Fraser, Allan, *Herd of the Hills*, T. &. A Constable Ltd., Edinburgh, 1934

Fraser, Allan, *Sheep Farming*, Crosby Lockwood & Son, London, 1937

Fraser, Allan, *Fiddler's Doom*, W. &. R. Chambers Ltd., Edinburgh, 1939

Fraser, Allan, *Sheep Husbandry*, Crosby Lockwood & Son, London, 1949

Gaskell, William, *Morvern Transformed*, Cambridge University Press, 1967

Grimble, Ian, *The Trial of Patrick Sellar*, Routledge and Kegan Paul, London, 1962

Gunn, Rev. Adam, 'Sutherland and the Reay Country', *Celtic Monthly*, Glasgow, 1897

Haldane, A.R.B., *The Drove Roads of Scotland*, Birlinn, Edinburgh, 1997

Hunter, James, *The Claim of Crofting*, Mainstream Publishing, Edinburgh, 1991

Hunter, James, *Last of the Free*, Mainstream Publishing, Edinburgh, 1999

Leneman, Leah, *Fit for Heroes?*, Aberdeen University Press, 1989

Macdonald, Colin, *Highland Memories*, The Moray Press, Edinburgh, 1949

Macvean, D.N. and Lockie, J.D., *Ecology and Land Use in Upland Scotland*, Edinburgh University Press, 1969

Mitchell, Joseph, *Reminiscences of my Life in the Highlands*, Vols I & 2, David and Charles Reprints, 1884

Mitchison, Rosalind, *Agricultural Sir John*, Geoffrey Bliss, London, 1962

Orr, Willie, *Deer Forests, Landlords and Crofters*, John Donald Publishers Ltd, 1982

Pearsall, W.H., *Mountains and Moorlands*, Collins, London, 1950

Phillips, John, *Moorland Management*, Quiller, Shrewsbury, 2012

Reader, John, *The Untold History of the Potato*, Vintage Books, London, 2009

Richards, Eric, *Patrick Sellar and the Highland Clearances*,
Polygon, Edinburgh, 1999

Richards, Eric and Clough, Monica, *Cromartie: Highland Life
1650–1914*, Aberdeen University Press, 1989

Sellar, Patrick, *Farm Reports. County of Sutherland*, Library of
Useful Knowledge, 1831

Sinclair, Sir John, *The Statistical Account of Scotland* Vol XVIII,
1791

Sinclair, Sir John, *The New Statistical Account of Scotland*,
William Blackwood & Sons Edinburgh, 1845

Slimon, Campbell, *Stells, Stools, Strupag*, Laggan Heritage,
2007

Smout, T.C. (ed), *Scotland since Prehistory*, Scottish Cultural
Press, Aberdeen, 1993

Stewart, Katharine, *Cattle on a Thousand Hills*, Luath Press,
Edinburgh, 2010

Tindley, Annie, 'The Iron Duke': land reclamation and public
relations in Sutherland, 1868–1895, *Historical Research*,
2009

Tindley, Annie, *The Sutherland Estate, 1850–1920: Aristocratic
Decline, Estate Management and Land Reform*, Edinburgh
University Press, 2010

Voisin, Andre, *Grass Productivity*, Crosby Lockwood & Son,
London, 1959

Appendix 1
The Clarke Family Tree c.1680–1921

The family of James Clarke, sometime tacksman of Clashneach in the parish of Durness.

John Clarke* c.1680–c.1730 (of whom little is known)

James Clarke* 1703–1774 Cnockbreac, Clashneach
m. Margaret Mackay 1726–1805 great-granddaughter of 1st Lord Reay

George	Barbara	Alexander	Donald	Robert	Hugh	Charles#	Mary	John*
Killed in		1760-	Both died in		1765-	1767-	1768	1770-
West Indies		1822	West Indies		1807	1831		1837
					John	Thomas	James	James
					James	Georgina	George	Georgina
					Robert	Hugh	Alexander	David
					Walter	James#	William	Alexander*
					Alexander	Margaret	Fairley	John
					Jane	Lucy	Eric	
					Janet	Robert	Margaret	
					John	Hugh	Mary	
					Hugh	Peggie	Hughina	
					Barbara	Dollie	Alexandrina	
					Kenneth	Barbara	Donald	
					Reay	Willina		
					Robina			

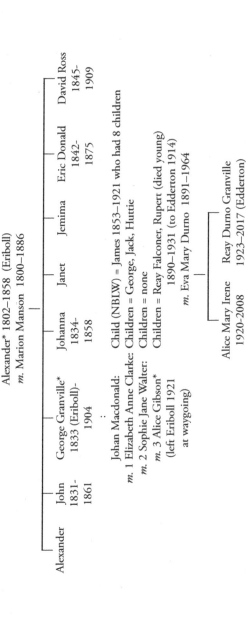

Tenants of Eriboll from 1815 to 1921 – and some of their descendants.

John* 1770–1837 (to Eriboll 1815)
m. Johanna Falconer 1774–1858

Alexander* 1802–1858 (Eriboll)
m. Marion Manson 1800–1886

| Alexander | John 1831–1861 | George Granville* 1833 (Eriboll)–1904 | Johanna 1834–1858 | Janet | Jemima | Eric Donald 1842–1875 | David Ross 1845–1909 |

Johan Macdonald:
m. 1 Elizabeth Anne Clarke:
m. 2 Sophie Jane Walter:
m. 3 Alice Gibson*
(left Eriboll 1921
at waygoing)

Child (NBIW) = James 1853–1921 who had 8 children
Children = George, Jack, Huttie
Children = none
Children = Reay Falconer, Rupert (died young)
1890–1931 (to Edderton 1914)
m. Eva Mary Durno 1891–1964

Alice Mary Irene
1920–2008

Reay Durno Granville
1923–2017 (Edderton)

Names thus:
John Clarke* (c1680–c1730), James,* John,* Alexander* and George Granville.* Each of these five so marked, plus Alice Gibson Clarke,* have a chapter in this book.

Charles# and (son) James# = each of the two so marked have a chapter in this book.

193

Appendix 2
The Sheep Stock on Eriboll: 1833, 1846, 1921 and 1983

The count of sheep on Eriboll over the past hundred and fifty years has been as follows. These figures must be treated with caution. Eriboll has changed in size.

1833: Clipping count. Eriboll: *c.*35,000 acres plus grazing on the Reay Forest

Ewes and gimmers:	2700
Wethers:	1500
Tups:	<u>69</u>
	<u>4269</u>

(This being a clipping count, the hoggs would have been counted as gimmers.)

1846: Clipping count. Eriboll: *c.*35,000 acres plus grazing on the Reay Forest

Total count:	5685 sheep

1921: Valuation count. Eriboll: *c.*30,000 acres

Ewes and gimmers:	3279
Ewe hoggs:	826
Wethers:	896
Tups:	<u>117</u>
	<u>5118</u>

1983: Sales brochure. Eriboll: 17,500 acres (Polla hirsel and land south of Cashel Dhu had been sold by this date.)

Ewes and gimmers:	2089
Ewe hoggs:	516
Tups:	<u>50</u> estimated
	<u>2655</u>

Appendix 3

Deterioration of the sward of a shieling when seasonal cattle grazing is changed to sheep farming

Herbage	Soil fauna	Soil	Birds and mammals
1. *Transhumant cattle with light mixed species grazing.*			
Clovers, grasses and shrubs, biologically rich and diverse	Many worms and invertebrates	Mull humus	Many seed and insect-eating birds, moles, voles, mice and predators
2. *After some years of continuous year-round grazing by sheep only.*			
Only low nutrient grasses	Few worms, few invertebrates	Becoming acidic, Low pH and phosphate	Fewer birds, few small mammals
3. *Continued year-round grazing by sheep only. Extensive muirburn.*			
Heather, Molinia	No worms, few invertebrates	Mor humus, Podsol forming	Some moorland birds, grouse, occasional red deer and predators
4. *A century and a half of continued year-round grazing by sheep only with occasional deer. Extensive muirburn.*			
Heather, Deer's Hair	Almost sterile	Iron pan forming, waterlogging	Few moorland birds, some nesting migrants, occasional red deer and predators
5. *Devastated terrain.*			

Notes:

1. The above is a suggestion as to what may happen to a shieling, which, in the past, has been grazed in summer by cattle plus a few sheep and goats and then becomes part of a sheep farm and is grazed throughout the year by a single species, sheep, and later by some deer. Underlying geology, slope, aspect and other factors will all affect the changes and speed at which such changes might occur.

2. The recycling of nutrients in the biological system will slow down very considerably, particularly with the loss of the dung from the cattle.

Acknowledgements
to the First (2014) Edition

The writing of this book started more than a decade ago as a result of a simple request from my four children that I should write down how long our family had farmed Eriboll. It was these same children, especially my daughter Janey, along with my late wife, Olga, who down the years have kept the project going and I am glad to be able to record my thanks to them. I would also like to thank my cousins, Mary Morrison and the late John and Walter Clarke, for a great deal of family background and family history.

Dr Malcolm Bangor-Jones has over the years sent me many extracts from documents on Eriboll and the Clarkes, which he came across during his researches. It was these that awakened my interest in my family's history. The result is this book, which I could not have written without his assistance. He also carefully went through the draft text and uncovered a host of glaring errors for me. I am very grateful to him. The late Geoffrey Baggott also sent me material of great interest which he discovered during his researches. I would indeed like to thank both these historians.

Professor Jim Hunter and Dr Annie Tindley have jointly written the foreword for this book* and have also given me valuable advice, encouragement and help just when it was most needed. Marlyn Price has prepared the maps, which are included in the book, with her usual skill and has ably dealt with the negotiations for copyrights. John Phillips of Laid and David Elliot of Rhigoulter have been most helpful in supplying information and talking through history, problems and difficulties. John Phillips also took a splendid collection of colour photographs of Eriboll

* Not in this edition.

for me of which four are reproduced in this book.* I am very grateful to him.

I would thank John Randall, the chairman of the Islands Book Trust, for undertaking the publication of this book and for all the help I have received from him, from the Trust, and from its members and its staff.

I am glad to have this opportunity to thank all these but it is to the hill shepherds of Sutherland, with whom I have worked, that I would especially wish to record my thanks. In particular these include the late Anson Mackay, the late Johnnie Mackay, the late Alec Beaton and the late Angus Cameron and there are many others. I just hope that a little of what I learnt from them of the herding of sheep on the hills of Sutherland has been faithfully recorded in this book.

Any errors or mistakes are entirely my responsibility.

Reay D. G. Clarke

* Not in this edition.